"Rev. Williams seeks to tak[...] and stereotypes to expose the reality of communities and people who have been neglected and abandoned by society. He tries to educate people on the realities of whole segments of our society who have been demonized and treated as throwaways. He reminds us that the good news of Jesus calls us not only to do the acts of charity that call us to care for our brothers and sisters but to demand justice and transform a society that has become comfortable with leaving brothers and sisters on the side of life's road."

Michael L. Pfleger, Faith Community of Saint Sabina, Chicago

"This book is fire! You will be moved to think and act differently, to meet people where they are, and join the resistance of God's people who refuse to accept injustice and apathy."

Shawn Casselberry, executive director of Mission Year

"After thirty-eight years of studying, living, and ministering in inner city Chicago, I recognize an authentic tour guide when I see one; they wear Jesus glasses, and they are incarnate and not in a car. Reverend Harry 'OG' Williams takes us to school with lessons from Oakland. His teachers are tenured by streets, courts, and prisons. Thank you, Harry Williams, for telling it like it is. We know that CCDA will empower some to stay and that is good, but what will urban ministry look like when the poor are scattered into the unincorporated collar counties distant from cities and community services?"

Ray Bakke, senior associate, Ray Bakke Associates, professor at Ray Bakke Centre for Urban Transformation, Hong Kong

"Real recognize real. OG Rev is a real one that has been serving some of the hardest parts of Oakland. *Taking It to the Streets* is a wake-up call for the church to go from apathy to compassion. It is filled with helpful insights and solutions for the future of the urban church."

Tommy "Urban D." Kyllonen, lead pastor, hip-hop artist, author of *Rebuild* and *Love Our City*

"Harry Williams has taken his years of work in the streets of Oakland and written a helpful and hopeful guide for those of us who know the gospel centers on the 'least of these.' Read these words carefully, but be warned: *Taking It to the Streets* is a rousing call to action from an 'OG Rev' that can't just be read but must be lived."

Jonathan Brooks, pastor, author of *Church Forsaken: Practicing Presence in Neglected Neighborhoods*

"I've walked the streets with my friend Harry 'Rev' Williams and know that he embodies the message of Jesus by living a life of radical, compassionate presence. This book is an urgent, gentle, lyrical, and prophetic invitation to let our hearts be broken, imagine a better future together, and join the resistance."

Mark Scandrette, author of *FREE, Belonging and Becoming,* and *Practicing the Way of Jesus*

TAKING

IT TO THE

HARRY LOUIS WILLIAMS II

LESSONS FROM A LIFE
OF URBAN MINISTRY

STREETS

ivp

An imprint of InterVarsity Press
Downers Grove, Illinois

InterVarsity Press
P.O. Box 1400, Downers Grove, IL 60515-1426
ivpress.com
email@ivpress.com

InterVarsity Press® is the book-publishing division of InterVarsity Christian Fellowship/USA®, a
movement of students and faculty active on campus at hundreds of universities, colleges, and schools
of nursing in the United States of America, and a member movement of the International Fellowship of
Evangelical Students. For information about local and regional activities, visit intervarsity.org.

All Scripture quotations, unless otherwise indicated, are taken from The Holy Bible, New International
Version®, NIV®. Copyright © 1973, 1978, 1984, 2011 by Biblica, Inc.™ Used by permission of Zondervan.
All rights reserved worldwide. www.zondervan.com. The "NIV" and "New International Version" are
trademarks registered in the United States Patent and Trademark Office by Biblica, Inc.™

While any stories in this book are true, some names and identifying information may have been
changed to protect the privacy of individuals.

Cover design and image composite: David Fassett
Interior design: Jeanna Wiggins
Images: black marble texture: © yokeetod / iStock / Getty Images Plus
　　　　white paper texture: © enjoynz / iStock / Getty Images Plus
　　　　holes in a wall: © Caspar Benson / Getty Images
　　　　gold texture background: © Katsumi Murouchi / Moment / Getty Images

ISBN 978-0-8308-4562-0 (print)
ISBN 978-0-8308-7265-7 (digital)

Printed in the United States of America ♾

InterVarsity Press is committed to ecological stewardship and to the conservation of natural
resources in all our operations. This book was printed using sustainably sourced paper.

Library of Congress Cataloging-in-Publication Data

Names: Williams, Harry Louis, author.
Title: Taking it to the streets : lessons from a life of urban ministry /
　Harry Louis Williams, II.
Description: Downers Grove, IL : InterVarsity Press, [2019] | Includes
　bibliographical references.
Identifiers: LCCN 2019013103 (print) | LCCN 2019019206 (ebook) | ISBN
　9780830872657 (eBook) | ISBN 9780830845620 (print : alk. paper) | ISBN
　9780830872657 (digital)
Subjects: LCSH: City missions—California—Oakland.
Classification: LCC BV2653 (ebook) | LCC BV2653 .W525 2019 (print) | DDC
　253.09173/2—dc23
LC record available at https://lccn.loc.gov/2019013103

P　25　24　23　22　21　20　19　18　17　16　15　14　13　12　11　10　9　8　7　6　5　4　3　2　1

Y　37　36　35　34　33　32　31　30　29　28　27　26　25　24　23　22　21　20　19

CONTENTS

 **INTRODUCTION**

H ave you ever seen a bullet-riddled body leaking blood on the asphalt of the church parking lot?

Have you ever been gripped by the chill of night as you watched a child being forced to sell her shivering, half-naked body in front of an empty church?

Have you ever watched hungry, homeless people, devoid of hope, wander sad-eyed up the streets and wondered why the church has not marshaled all its terrific resources to put bread in their bellies?

I have.

A spirit of indifference has gripped God's local body by its throat. A blindness to the suffering of the most vulnerable people around us has set in. Lethargy has attached itself to the body like a malignant disease feeding on its host. Apathy has attacked the core of who we are as believers.

I remember the day when I came to understand the dark truth of the matter. A few years ago, two gang members in a car spotted rivals walking down a bustling Oakland, California, street in the middle of a summer day. A pistol swung out of the window, and one of the gangstas pointed at a figure in the crowd of shoppers, ready to blow his enemy's head off. He fired. The thing was, he missed. The stray bullet pierced through a baby carriage and struck a toddler. The child died instantly.

In the aftermath, the streets of East Oakland were awash with tears. I remember watching elementary school children, barely having mastered their ABCs, marching down the sidewalks near the scene of the killing holding up cardboard signs that said, "Don't Shoot Me!" and "I'm Too Young to Die!"

In the wake of the killing, I sat down with a local pastor and told him how difficult homicide and gun violence were making it for people who lived in the community that he was sworn to protect. I will never forget his response: "It's not as bad as you're making it." His words astonished me. I was speechless. To my overwhelming sense of wonder, many faith leaders took his viewpoint.

What dark forces allowed them to be so completely unmoved by the plight of the people? In their eyes I saw the apathy, the disinterest, the dispassionate disregard for the ones Jesus called "the least of these." Apathy is a silent killer. It is the demonic assassin that destroys churches, rotting their innards like termites burrowing through the walls of a wooden doll house. Apathy causes us to throw polite, spiritual quips and quotes on a situation that has landed like a tsunami in the ghettoes of North America.

To defeat this tsunami, a resistance must be mounted. What must be resisted? Apathy! For believers to address some of the complex problems that face urban America, it is going to take passion, fire, and commitment. It's going to take guts. It is going to take the power of the risen Christ.

The death of Lazarus is one of the most memorable passages in the New Testament. Upon hearing of his good friend's illness, Jesus does not budge from his location. By the time he finally starts in

2

Lazarus's direction, Lazarus is dead. When he arrives at Bethany, Lazarus's sister Martha greets Jesus with these words: "Lord, if you had been here, my brother would not have died. But I know that even now God will give you whatever you ask" (John 11:21-22).

Just as in Jesus' day, a resurrection is needed. We can look at the body and holler "Come alive" until the next solar eclipse. However, it will take the power of God to breathe life into the body. We can massage the heart and blow breath into nostrils, but we must trust God to do the work of resurrection in those places where apathy has turned the flesh blue. We need this resurrection to occur because there are so many in America's 'hood who know the Almighty's name only as a cuss word. We've never gone to them to explain what we've seen, learned, and experienced of God. Oh, that the Lord would give us the thirst to take his message to the streets!

STEP FOOT IN THE RESISTANCE

Where do you come in? When you decided to follow Jesus, you exited from the freshly paved freeway that led to comfort and safety. You are now on the narrow road with the signposts above that read "Do or Die" and "Pick Up Your Cross Here." This new life demands all. Daily it calls for commitment. Daily it calls for sacrifice. Daily it calls out from Scriptures to put God first, others second. This hierarchy is at the center of the resistance.

Jesus died an enemy of the state, crucified between two thieves and with a sign over his head that read "King of the Jews." Jesus lived a radical life, and the call to follow him has never been one of ease and tranquility. The question is, are you going to follow this radical Jesus? I mean really follow him? Are you prepared to go all the way, or is your faith just another box to check off like membership to your lodge, your Greek fraternal organization, or your favorite sports team?

Pastor, are you seeking to be a righteous revolutionary, or are you willing to settle for the role of religious cruise-ship director? Churches are dying all over America's inner cities because they no longer point to the commitment that life in Christ demands. They host weekly services. Some still draw large numbers. However, they are no longer lighthouses for those in darkness. Inside, they are empty husks and pretty corpses. There is no passion left to compel the lost to life and no power left to fight the darkness. The members are merely going through the motions of some sort of socioemotional catharsis. It's no longer real, if ever it was. Let me tell you about what it means to be real in these streets.

REAL IN THE FIELD

When a gangster nods in your direction and says, "Oh, he's solid!" you have arrived. If your ambition is to achieve royalty in the criminal underworld, at that moment you can consider yourself good to go. To have the right person say, "She's about that life" or to use words like *reputable* or *real* in connection to your name is the equivalent of having the late Stephen Hawking proclaim you an astrophysics visionary. In a world where all you have is your name, authenticity is priceless. To be called any of those names is to say that you're not an internet banger or studio gangster. Both feet are firmly planted in the lifestyle of the block, no looking back. People in the 'hood measure faith and faith institutions by the same yard stick. How committed are you to ministry in the killing fields?

Sure, you'll hear a lot of singing when you enter most churches located in the inner city. Hands will clap in rhythm to choruses like "This Little Light of Mine." You may feel like marching as great anthems of the church like "Onward Christian Soldiers" are lifted up. The pastor may even preach a rousing sermon exhorting his members to love your neighbor as yourself. But how will any of that translate into the church body's relationship with the most impoverished members of the community around the church building or across town? How will the light that was sung about illuminate the courtyard of the trailer park or the housing projects? Will the Christian soldiers be marching into the gang war to assure the besieged and beleaguered that God is concerned for them? And that message about loving one's neighbor as oneself . . .

And yet it is real. I have seen the dazzling light twinkle in the eyes of men and women of God who wander the killing fields seeking someone to accept their prayer. I'll never be too spiritual to ask for that prayer. I want to hear them read the Scriptures underlined in their well-worn Bibles. I tap my feet to the acapella style. They have come here to meet us, the weary and the hard pressed, saints and sinners.

THE HARVEST

Jesus said, "The harvest is plentiful but the workers are few" (Matthew 9:37). Here's what I found interesting as I recently considered that Scripture. Jesus lived in a world populated with Sadducees, Pharisees, and scribes. In his sojourn through the dusty streets of ancient Galilee, Jesus is constantly running into these religious figures. Time after time, he argues with them in the synagogue or the temple; occasionally he finds himself reclined across from them at a dinner table. There seems to be no shortage of high priests or Levites in Jesus' world. How then, could he possibly say that the laborers are few? The answer is quite simple: they did not routinely perform activities in the redemptive and healing works of almighty God.

Ministry has not changed much over the years. Religion is often an elaborate masquerade, and not everybody wearing a uniform or a name badge is necessarily going to work in the harvest field. Just like in ancient Israel, the harvest fields of inner-city America are brimming over and crying out for authentic believers who are committed to bringing the message and touch of Jesus Christ to the masses. People lost in the streets are searching not so much for orthodox church members as members of the resistance—Jesus-followers who are not going to trip when people come into the church with their pants sagging or the scent of marijuana emanating from their clothes. They are looking for believers who aren't afraid to greet them on the avenue, and ask how they are doing and mean it.

WHERE DO YOU START?

Matthew 20:29-34 recounts the story of two men on the side of a dusty road in ancient Palestine. Though sightless, they can hear the excitement as the great teacher and healer who has become rather famous in their world draws close. They call out to Jesus. The crowd, thinking Jesus is too important to take up time with these men, tells the men to quiet down. Undaunted, they cry out all the louder. Finally, Jesus asks, "What do you want me to do?" They answer, "We want our sight."

Jesus touches the men and heals their vision. However, before this great miracle is performed, we find one of the most poignant phrases in the Scriptures: "Jesus had compassion on them."

I urge you to look up the word *compassion* in the Gospels. You will find that every time Jesus is moved with compassion, a miracle occurs. Compassion is more than someone looking at tragedy and saying, "Aw, isn't that too bad?" Jesus had unspeakable empathy. When Jesus experienced compassion, he was moved in his guts, in the very core of his being, by the plight of the person in front of him. When Jesus was filled with compassion, he responded with all of his power to meet the need.

Compassion is the opposite of apathy. Compassion is the fuel of the resistance. It is the heart that beats for the other. Compassion compels us to the streets.

Be filled with compassion. Let it envelop you. Let it encircle you. Let it surround you. Let it pour through the membranes of your skin. Let it glow in the pupils of your eyes. Be like Jesus. Let compassion be the prevailing force behind your motives and movements.

Compassion will press you to find answers that must be searched through late-night study. It will force you to go beyond what some might think reasonable. Compassion is the godly grace that will press like the hands of God on your back when you are tired and the situation appears hopeless.

If you want to be successful in urban mission, godly compassion is not the only tool you'll need, but it well may be the essential one. If you possess it, you won't have to tell anyone. Everyone will see it. Compassion will help you to make sense of what you're about to read. You need it. If you don't possess it in measure, you must crave it. Pray for it.

In the coming pages, I will take you face to face with some deep problems that confront people in the inner cities. Some of you will be startled to find out that people in the United States live in such squalor, deprivation, and hunger. You may even be tempted to put this book down and stick your head back in the sand. I want to encourage you to resist that urge and keep reading. However, instead of reading this book like a theologian or a sociologist, I want you to put on what I call your "Jesus glasses." Look at the world I'm laying out for you through the lenses of Christ's compassion. Pray that God will peel away the layers of unseen apathy that might hinder you from seeing his children as Jesus sees them.

Remember apathy is the great enemy of our cause. It must be resisted. We need to strip it off like grave clothing. Have you chosen to do so? Then welcome to the underground network of believers called the "resistance." Let's take it to the streets.

THE RESISTANCE IS REAL

Welcome to My 'Hood

I n a war, an underground resistance is a tiny group of dissidents that rises up behind enemy lines with the intent of overthrowing the empire. Often the resistance movement is composed of bakers, newspaper writers, bankers, housewives, bus drivers, college students, retirees—regular people fed up with the status quo. They don't carry banners and flags. They go about their work silently but with great resolve beating in their hearts. When history is written, we find that the war could not have been won without the courage and willingness of a tiny resistance party to put it all on the line for the cause.

You don't have to be a great orator to serve this modern-day faith resistance. You don't need a graduate school degree or ordination papers to be part of the resistance. You need compassion and a heart surrendered to Jesus Christ. I have met members of the resistance who change diapers in the church nursery, pick up children for Sunday school, mentor inner-city youth, and hand out food in tent cities. Are you prepared to love as Jesus loved? Are you prepared to take this all the way? Are you

11

prepared to resist apathy and to walk in the lifestyle of Christlike compassion? Then let's go.

KICKING IT WITH O.G. REV

At this point, I want you to use your sanctified imagination. It is a cool, California summer day. You've just landed in Oakland. The instructions you've received lead you to a public park on East 86th Avenue where you find a middle-aged cat with salt and pepper hair wearing a T-shirt that says, "O.G. Rev." (That would be me.) I am sipping an eight-ounce bottle of orange-flavored Perrier water. I'm nodding my head to an obscure Wu-Tang Clan song playing in my headphones. I am deeply immersed in a book titled *The Dead Emcee Scrolls*, by poet Saul Williams.

The music is super loud, but when I look up from the book, I think I can almost read your lips. Did you say, "Brother man, apathy has turned the whole situation into an icicle. It seems as though the whole faith community is rolling with the status quo. What can be done?"

Allow me to introduce myself. In the streets, they call me O.G. Rev or Rev for short. Consider me your O.G. homie. Not familiar with that term? Let me break it down for you. O.G. stands for "original gangster." Since nothing in the 'hood is ever exactly what it looks or sounds like, let's go in a little deeper. An O.G. is not necessarily a career criminal, though they might have a colorful past. An O.G. might have at one time or another been a gang member infamous for putting in that work (as they say), aiming an Uzi out of the window of a rust bucket Ford Pinto and showering hot shells on rivals. An O.G. might have spent a decade or two in a California concrete slave ship. After this person has lived long enough to outrun their past, in semiretirement they become known as an O.G., a respected (or feared) veteran of the block.

Relax, I'm not that kind of O.G., though I am a veteran of the same streets. Over the years, my mission hasn't been to sling dope but to give hope. My goal has not been to leave rivals dead in a puddle of blood but to preach eternal life through the shed blood of Jesus Christ and his resurrection. I know O.G.s who can disassemble an AK-47 like a Green Beret, and my aim is to be able to take apart a Bible in much the same way. What I have in common with your traditional O.G. homie is that as a minister to the 'hood, we are both out in these streets to influence the same people.

Stare through the dark tint of my Loc sunglasses. Can you see the reflection of this lost world in my eyes? These eyes have seen oceans of tears and rivers of blood. These eyes have seen kids with snotty noses dancing in the rain as their addicted parents sit in dark apartments without gas or electricity sticking needles into their burnt-out veins.

Can you see the reflection of this lost world in my eyes? These eyes have seen so many of my brothers herded in chains to live till they die in the California concrete slave ships, toiling like tortured slaves for less than twenty cents an hour.

Can you see the reflection of this lost world in my eyes? These eyes have seen pastors in luxury sedans flying through the mayhem and rubbish, taking corners on two wheels, racing behind iron gates to preach the Word of the Lord, Bible and collection plate in hand. Yeah, man. What I've seen through these two eyes is enough to make your brain twist in your skull. I am your O.G. homie.

Why do you need an O.G. homie if you want to do ministry in the streets? Pretty much for the same reason that a hoodlum intent on learning the game needs a seasoned mentor. In the 'hood, the toss of the head or a slang term can have two or three different meanings. The same playful joke that might make you the life of the party in the suburbs might land you at the wrong end of a pistol in a place where people live close to the edge. Someone with life experience as an insider on the streets will probably be able to help you both optimize your ministry effectiveness and avoid some terrible pitfalls.

In *The Mack*, a famous blaxploitation movie of the 1970s, Max Julien plays Goldie, a young pimp set on making a fortune from the Oakland streets. One of the most powerfully drawn characters in the film is a blind man with jet-black sunglasses. He's an older cat who sits on a stool in the back of the pool hall day after day, a former hustler who has experienced a run of bad luck but still ventures out of the house suited and booted to take his perch in the den of iniquity. He has few lines. In fact, I'm not even sure he has a name. He might sit there motionless every day amid the cigarette clouds and profanity, but his ears are capturing everything. He is Goldie's crime mentor. He whispers priceless insider information about the dark doings and goings on in the underworld into Goldie's ear. For the next two hundred pages, I'm going to be your sanctified version of the hoodlum in the pool hall with the jet-black shades.

Kick back. Relax. We're underground now. We are not easy to find, but there is a movement afoot, and it only takes two sticks to start a fire. Welcome to the resistance. Now, focus in and let me lace your boots. (Translated: Let me share some knowledge with you.)

FUNERAL FOR A HUSTLER

If you are caught up in a lifestyle that makes it impractical to walk outside of your house without a gun tucked in your belt, the odds of long life are against you. One young man's life had simply expired. Oakland is only so big. It's not a metropolis of millions like Chicago or New York City. If you have enemies on these streets, it's only a matter of time before you meet up at the same gas station or a crowded McDonald's. And if you do dirt out in these streets (translated: rob people, steal drugs, pimp somebody's daughter, violate someone's family, break into the wrong person's house, etc.), you can expect to meet the fiery end of a pistol sooner than later.

This young man in the box had received his share of warnings. Words of caution came from his cousins, his siblings, his mother, even his enemies. And yet his addiction to the fast money, street fame, and lure of darkness kept him chained to the block. One day a gangsta caught him slipping (translated: to be caught unaware or not paying attention to one's surroundings) at a red light and emptied an AK-47 clip in his chest.

His family grieved as I read Psalm 23 at the funeral. I took a moment to look down into the white box at my feet. My, he looked young. He looked even younger than his twenty-something years. I had been in this spot before—different day, different body, same situation. And each time I stood behind that pulpit lectern, the same thoughts came to me: Homicide is so widespread in our community, why don't Christians take the dramatic loss of black life more seriously? Where are the pastors? Why isn't there screaming in the streets? Where is the outcry? Why doesn't the world simply stop to acknowledge the tragedy of another young life lost?

Looking back at the young man in the casket, I had more questions. Why didn't believers mount a full-scale initiative to reach him when he was a child, long before he wound up a street figure looking down the wrong end of an assault rifle?

Every Sunday, people in the 'hood drove past him to go worship Jesus. Why didn't somebody stop to invite him to church? That's one of those questions we may have to answer on the great Day of Judgment. However, if I had to venture a guess, I would have to say that our sense of compassion has frozen over.

When Cain murdered his brother, God said that Abel's blood called out to him from the ground. Abel was one person. How many thousands of Abels have perished by gunfire in the streets of America's 'hoods in the past forty years? The cry of blood must be deafening, like tropical thunder, in God's ears. But does it stir us? That's the question. It seems we are more concerned about repaving the parking lot or filling the pastor's anniversary offering than who the coroner is carting away at the end of the block. Something has gone wildly wrong in the household of faith. Apathy has turned us cold as a stone.

When a natural disaster occurs in America, the flags fly at half-staff. However, when hundreds and hundreds of people are murdered in cities chock-full of churches, there is no day of mourning. Why not? Apathy. It is one of Satan's greatest weapons of war.

APATHY IS CHOKING THE LIFE OUT OF US

During the Montgomery bus boycott, Rev. Dr. Martin Luther King Jr. was preaching at a local church when he noticed several members of his church whispering with worried looks on their faces. Immediately, he called them up to the front of the church. It turns out that segregationists had just bombed the parsonage while King's wife and baby were inside. King rushed home, not knowing what he'd find. Sure enough, the front of his house had been blown up. Thank God, his wife, Coretta Scott King, and his infant daughter had been in a back room.

King later said that he felt his faith and resolve wavering at that point. However, he never turned back. And we all know how the boycott turned out. Where is that kind of courage today? Where is our conviction for the least and the left out? Make no mistake about it, it's going to take the level of courage that King had (and more) to wage war against the enemy in a place where the price of human life is cheap and falling by the day.

I participate in many marches for a variety of different causes. They are never easy for me. You see, I have short legs and flat feet, and I walk slower than most people. Some months back, I participated in a "Stop the Violence" march. Eventually, I found myself at the end of the processional. There was one woman there, the mother of two sons. She too was a slow walker. We became fast friends. I asked, "Mother, what brought you out to this march?"

"One of my sons got arrested on a minor infraction," she said. "When they took him into custody, a cop asked if he had a brother. He told him he did. His younger brother hadn't been home in a couple of days. We were afraid. We didn't know what had happened to him. As it turned out, my son in custody looked so much like his brother that the cop saw the resemblance and told him they had a deceased John Doe in a coroner's locker that he wanted him to look at. Sure enough, it was my other son."

As it turns out, my new friend's younger son had gone to visit a girl in another part of the city. She had set him up. Gang members jumped on him, robbed him, and left him for dead. His mother told of the tears, the brokenness, and the anguish that had wracked her life in the wake of her son's passing.

"I get involved in anything that helps stops the violence because it stops me from losing my mind," she said.

I wish I could tell you that this woman's misfortune was some sort of anomaly, but it's not. In the wake of the mass killings of young black men across the nation, mothers weep. Children walk to apartment windows at night and stare down at the sidewalk, waiting for a father who will never come home.

Some urban churches have a policy that prevents homicide funerals from being held in their buildings. And in many churches, the local pastor will not discuss the fallen during the Sunday sermon. As far as many believers are concerned, the deceased could be just another lifeless body thrown on top of a trash heap on the outskirts of town. We label the lost as troublesome, even loathsome, if we even stop to think of their short lives at all. Apathy has turned off the light switch of concern. That's why we need a spiritually based resistance movement to help us recapture the teachings and practice of Jesus.

HEARING THE CALL

The witness of the traditional church has dimmed. In many instances the warriors for social justice who led the civil rights movement have failed to pass the torch to the younger generation. The great infusion of cash into the Christian pastorate has made some of the potential warlords for holiness and justice too complacent to lead the battle for life and survival into the blood-soaked streets of America's Golgothas. They are now sliding on the greased boards of prosperity down to the pits of irrelevancy, their congregations in tow. I'm not telling you something I've read in a book. I know a bunch of these ministers on a firsthand basis. I have shaken their slick hands. I have watched the gleam in their eyes as the offering basket shifted from hand to hand. Thank God, they do not represent the benediction to our story.

When I first came to Oakland, I taught at a small Christian college in a drug-drenched war zone. The sounds of sirens and gunshots created a raucous symphony of revenge and bloodshed. The grim reaper stalked the streets, cutting down young bodies with a razor-sharp, bloody scythe. In the middle of it marched some of my young students, Bibles tucked beneath their arms. They went door-to-door asking the besieged residents if they wanted prayer. I remember one neighbor beckoning us into her house like we were firefighters summoned to her home to battle a five-alarm blaze. There are people like her all over the inner-city mission field, their faces practically pressed against the window glass, waiting for help to show up.

God is calling servants into America's 'hoods. A few years ago, a young woman contacted me and said she felt the call of God to serve young people in the 'hoods of San Francisco. She wanted to meet with me the next time she was in the city. She lived out of town—way out of town. In fact, she lived on another continent. All the way on that foreign shore, she felt God press on her heart to reach her arms around people in one of San Francisco's most depressed communities. Do you know where she is today? She lives in San Francisco and serves the people of that community. The resistance is real.

WHEN THE SPIRIT HAS MOVED ON

The prophet Elijah once became discouraged at what seemed to be the collapse of his nation's support for the true and living God. "And what was God's answer to him? 'I have reserved for myself seven thousand who have not bowed the knee to Baal'" (Romans 11:4).

Today, members of the resistance grow weary like Elijah because they are looking for God in places where God has been kicked out and subsequently has moved on. We are looking for the God of creation in the innovations of yesteryear, and God is no longer there. God is creative. God is somewhere else doing new things in new places.

Years ago, a good friend invited me to keep him company while he cleaned a large church built in colonial times in an East Coast city. Even though the church was hundreds of years old, it had been maintained well and was in pristine condition. I estimated that the structure could have seated a thousand people comfortably. When I asked my friend, the church janitor, approximately how many people had attended the previous Sunday, he looked up from his vacuuming and, with a whimsical smile, said, "Maybe fifty."

He said, "Harry, if they didn't start renting this place out to other churches, it would have closed down long ago."

Apparently, a handful of members still trekked there because they saw the church as part of their family legacy. They didn't want to have it said that the place ceased to exist on their watch.

I looked at the beautiful Romanesque white columns and the ornate stained-glass windows and asked myself, *How can it be dead?* But it was. It didn't matter that they still met; the spark of divinity had left the assembly. The neighbors in the vastly changed community that now surrounds the building were hollering, "Flatline!"

The numbers mean nothing. A church can be alive and blossoming spiritually with ten members or dead with ten thousand. The question: Is the assembly hungry not only to grow in spiritual knowledge but also to serve the people right outside its doors—the impoverished, the disinherited, the spiritually famished? If so, the day is going to come when methods change even as motives and message remain the same.

In inner cities all over the country, God is doing a new thing. Luke 5:36-39 says,

> [Jesus] told them this parable: "No one tears a piece out of a new garment to patch an old one. Otherwise, they will have torn the new garment, and the patch from the new will not match the old. And no one pours new wine into old wineskins. Otherwise, the new wine will burst the skins; the wine will run out and the wineskins will be ruined. No, new wine must be poured into new wineskins. And no one after drinking old wine wants the new, for they say, 'The old is better.'"

I believe in my soul that we are merely looking at the gleam of the morning sun on the horizon. Something powerful is headed this way. God has heard so many prayers that God's response is coming. Will you be a part of this new movement of God's Spirit? Are you ready to take it the streets?

HOMEWORK

- Write a two thousand-word essay on this topic: What is apathy? Where do we see it in ministry? How has it impacted urban ministry?

- What would it mean to mount a resistance? What would a resistance look like?

CHILDREN OF THE STREETS

The High Price of Apathy

So far, I have laid out two powerful abstractions: apathy and resistance. Now I want to lay out some concrete issues that need to be addressed. People will live and die based on which of those two abstractions are applied to the situations you are about to discover. I will tell you about a world that you might not have seen before. I will introduce you to its children. Let me take you back to an experience I had a few weeks ago. Read closely.

YOUNG AND IN REAL DANGER

She might be the mayor one day, I thought as I watched the glimmer in her onyx-colored eyes. Her head nodded up and down at every sentence as I read from a book about the sit-in movement of the 1960s. She was visualizing the story. It was like I was reading a movie to her. She was ten years old. Surrounding her were about twenty other students. Some were just as engaged as the little girl with the onyx eyes. One child on the other side of the room would not let me finish a page without shooting her hand in the air with a question. "Mr. Harry," she asked at one point, "Why didn't they want the slaves to know how to read?"

Teaching young people is sacred work. You are putting fingerprints in the fresh soil of young minds. You are helping someone build the conscious reality of the world around them. You are handing the building blocks for their future dreams. I was at that inner-city elementary school for but a single hour to read a passage from a book as part of the Black History Month celebration. However, in that hour I noticed that not all of the young people were as engaged as those brilliant young people seated near the front of the room.

One young girl with a fist-sized hole in the knee of her blue jeans nodded off, desperately trying to get the sleep that had evaded her the night before. She looked weary, older. Another young boy raised his hand when I asked questions only to respond with the word, "Cookies!" He was disruptive, purposefully so. Yet he was not doing so to be mean. Well-behaved or not, each child modeled a reflection of their home life.

Take the brilliant little girl with the onyx eyes. It was obvious that someone had invested a great deal of time and care in her presentation to the world that morning. Her hair was carefully combed and greased and placed into a bun. Her clothes were clean and pressed.

Some of the other children were not quite as fortunate. One boy looked as though he had slept in the same outfit he wore to school. While most of the children were focused on the story book about the civil rights movement, another child raised his hand and asked for legal advice for his father, an incarcerated felon facing his third strike.

At the end of the hour, I bid the students farewell and headed out the door with all kinds of thoughts colliding in my mind. As I looked back on the faces of those young people, I realized that some of them were being groomed for success. They had parents or caretakers who were invested in making sure they ate nutritious food, slept for eight or nine hours a night in a comfortable place, and had all the support they needed to be successful in school. And then there were other kids, just as intellectually gifted but not born into stability. Some had drug-addicted parents, if their parents were present at all. Some were homeless, shifting from one relative's couch to another. Some lived in trap houses (apartments where people come and go day and night to buy and use drugs). These are challenging circumstances in which to engage in homework assignments.

They all looked so young. Yet, in seven or eight years, each one of those young people will be adults. Some will be putting their promise to work in college. Some will be joining the workforce. And others might well become the addicted and the broken sleeping in tents and counted among the homeless on the back streets and alleys of the city.

God bless the children.

KIDS ON LOCKDOWN

A few days later, I met with a group in another inner-city institution for youth. They looked like tiny eighteenth-century slaves in ill-fitting khaki suits as they were paraded into the day room escorted by jail guards. Their heads were uncombed, their faces devoid of the light that comes from basking in the glow of the sun. I took a seat and waited. Jack Bryson had invited me here tonight.

Jack leads a coalition of community folks and police officers who are fighting to improve their relationship in the community. Monthly, they stage meetings at local barbershops where community folks can air their grievances with the police. This night, they decided to have that conversation behind bars at a juvenile detention facility. We were asked to sit with one incarcerated child on each side. A little biracial girl who looked like she would be more at home on the soccer field of a suburban high school than here in warrior camp sat on one side of me. A light-skinned boy with eyes that reflected his intense thirst to get out of that place sat on the other side.

A number of powerful speakers were scheduled to tell their stories that night including my friend Mr. Butler, a police officer turned drug dealer who did two decades in the iron house for murder. This former high-ranking drug dealer said that concerned local police officers once asked him what it would take to exit the game. When he answered "a job," they helped him find one, which turned his life around. Rappers were there. Even a few NFL athletes came there unannounced and without the fanfare of TV cameras. Each had the heart to want to save this room full of youth and their families from a lifetime of misery and incarceration.

At one point, a young boy with a flattop haircut was put on the spot. He was instructed to rise to his feet and tell the crowd what he had learned from the myriad of voices he had heard that night. His answer was succinct but poignant: "To succeed, you have to have a plan for when you get out of here." All of us clapped, but a young female inmate went even further. Before anyone could respond, she jumped up from her seat and ran over to the young man speaking and threw her arms around him. He was her brother. They were both locked up in the same facility at the same time, albeit in different units.

As he took his seat, I looked to the little girl on my right and I asked, "What did you learn, my sister?" She said, "You gotta have a plan. And you also gotta watch your friends. My friends got me put in here, and ain't a one of them get arrested when the cuffs got slapped on me."

At the conclusion of the evening, we went around to shake hands and speak words of encouragement to the youth. As I looked into the eyes of the kids and offered my most powerful words of motivation, I was struck by the thought that the experience of incarceration would not deter some of them from the lure of the streets. Sure, some would make it, but many will know the stench and coldness of the penitentiary.

Again that night as we parted from those children, I wondered about the witness of the Christian community to these at-risk kids. Are there churches who reach out to these young people, offering them Jesus and a place in a loving faith community upon their return to society? Or do we simply leave them as prey for the wolves and coyotes who prowl the back streets of the 'hood with nothing to lose? As I watched at those children with ill-fitting, state-issued clothing and broken footwear scamper out of sight, I wondered why there was no protracted faith struggle to save them.

JESUS LOVES THE CHILDREN

One of the most popular Christian children's songs is "Jesus Loves the Little Children." Jesus loved children. He had an affection for all of the most vulnerable members of his creation. Jesus embraced their innocence.

The Gospels tell the story of a gaggle of young children who run toward Jesus to be blessed. The disciples are irate. They chase the children away, saying that Jesus is too busy for them. In direct opposition, Jesus summons the young ones back to himself. He lays hands on them and blesses them. I wonder what kind of prayers Jesus prayed for those kids. Did he pray for their health? Did he pray for success in their future careers? Did he pray that they would have adequate food and shelter?

If Jesus had been born in the twenty-first century instead of the first, what kind of blessings might flow through his hands as he prays for children in the 'hood today? What kind of things might he ask as he intercedes on their behalf before God? What type of needs might Jesus feel compelled to respond to if he was walking the concrete blocks of an American inner-city today? I'll take it a step further. Since I minister in the San Francisco Bay Area, I want to take you to a place I saw a few days ago and ask you to see it through Christ's eyes. What would he see? What might Jesus do?

Cold rain spat down on us from thick, angry clouds that circled around tall gray buildings. It was chilly for the Bay Area that day. Tourists and business people marched up and down the Powell Street hill, a steep asphalt mountain perfect for a toboggan run had it been in Austria or Alaska. The street cars made famous in the Rice-A-Roni commercial clanged back and forth along the rails in the middle of the street.

This street is a panhandler's paradise. If you are collecting coins, you want to go where thousands of unsuspecting tourists and out-of-towners might show some generosity.

A tension knot bunched up in my stomach when I came across them. He was a tall man with long hair. Beside him was a baby carriage. The blue canvas hood was stretched over a child who lay still beneath a clump of light blue blankets.

Laid out on the sidewalk next to them was a piece of cardboard with an impassioned plea for help. In front of the sign was a cup filled with a few one-dollar bills.

I did a double take, but I wasn't alone. This child was not a human being as much as he was a begging prop. Was that his father or just a neighbor borrowing the boy, who appeared to be about two years old, for a fundraising expedition? Drugs are a terrible thing. After a few years of chemical enslavement, there is no bottom left and no line you won't cross for one more hit. At the end of the money trail lies a toddler with rain water and tears washing his face. The man with the child does not have an umbrella to ward off the raindrops. That's on purpose. He wants to dramatize the child's plight. The toddler's discomfort will result in more bucks in the cup from horrified tourists from Eastern Europe, Japan, and Canada.

Sadly enough, ain't nobody coming to save this toddler. The man with the dreads knows the law. As long as he keeps the canopy over the child, as long as the wet blankets surround the child's body, the authorities have no cause to get involved. As the baby stares out at the cold world, his tiny fingers cold to the touch, dark seeds grow in his soul.

With a start in life like this, it would be a miracle if he found his way to college. The reality is, before he can even walk he's on his way to jail. Yes, the cradle-to-prison pipeline is real. Everyday America gives birth to throwaway kids like the little boy lying in wet blankets on a rainy day. Along his path to adulthood, he'll meet plenty of black and brown kids who share his unsavory journey to what, God only knows.

LOST CHILDREN

No, America is not the land of equality for all, especially as pertaining to its children.

In her book *Power Concedes Nothing: One Woman's Quest for Social Justice*, lawyer Constance Rice writes about a visit she once had with a room full of gang members in Los Angeles's Nickerson Gardens Housing Projects. Each of the young men was introduced to her by name except for a small boy with golden brown skin and curlicue hair who sat alone in the corner.

One of the men looked at the little boy Rice calls Pygmy and says, "Tell the lady what you do for a livin'."[1]

The little boy's face went blank. It had no affect at all. He said, "I kill." As the conversation continued, she realized that she was looking at a nine-year-old assassin conscripted into war by the men Rice disparagingly calls the "satanic six." "Yeh. I kill people—who they tell me," he said, referring to the gang members.

The nine-year old knew too many details to be making this story up. She remarks, "But it was his soulless eyes that bared the truth. Pygmy had died with his targets. I was talking to a child soldier."

She asked herself, "What kind of toxic indifference had spawned this outrage? It should not have been possible—not anywhere in the richest country the planet has ever known."

Who was Pygmy? Both of his parents were incarcerated shortly after he was born. In those times, according to Rice, it was not uncommon for LAPD to arrest adults and leave the children alone without notifying County Child Services. There was no record of the nine-year-old's birth. He was passed from one gang-affiliated relative to another until he was lost to the streets. Where is he now? Only Jesus knows.

Spike Lee's movie *Chi-Raq* starred John Cusack in the role of an inner-city priest driven to stop the killings in Chicago. Cusack's character was based on a real-life hero, Father Michael Pfleger of St. Sabina's Church on Chicago South Side. Pfleger said in an interview with Dr. Boyce Watkins,

> We always link abortion to something that goes on in a womb in a clinic. If we believe that every human being has a God-given purpose and destiny, then anything, anything that cuts short that person from reaching that destiny, that divine purpose—that's a form of abortion. . . . So bad education is abortion. No jobs are abortion. Racism is abortion. Poverty is abortion. . . . Let's stop aborting these kids out here. Abortion doesn't end in conception. Abortion ends when they die. . . . Let's stop aborting these kids by putting them in prison or hanging on the corner out in the streets. Let's help them reach their dreams. Let's love them. Let's care about them. Let's help them.[2]

I first became aware of author and filmmaker Dashaun "Jiwe" Morris when I picked up his riveting book *War of the Bloods in My Veins*. It traces his journey as a child from a troubled, inner-city home to his perch high above a Bloods gang empire in Newark, New Jersey. He has unique insight into inner-city trauma that the best-trained sociologists lack. While writing this book, I came across a post on his Facebook page. It fit perfectly into the point I wanted to make in this chapter. I wrote to him, and he graciously allowed me to reprint it. Read carefully:

Do you know how many kids grow up gutter, crack babies because the daddy's a gangster who promotes violence? The kid has no boundaries, no home life, no discipline, no role model, except the killers. There's no order in his life. He goes to bed many nights malnourished and hasn't eaten a proper breakfast, lunch or dinner in years. He hasn't seen the dentist in years. He drinks soda and juice and eats candy all day. Mom doesn't have the tools to raise him because she's hooked on snow white [cocaine] and he sees her pipes and needles laid out in the house. There are men coming in and out. But we expect him to go to 3rd grade class and focus on Science, English, Math while this lil dude flashin' images of mama all foamed at d f—in' mouth, and he can't seem to fight back tears.

U wonder why he got his first kill at 14 and u say but how? Death has been celebrated his whole 14 yrs of life. He sees praise bein' thrown at the older guys when they recall kill missions. Dat lil dude doesn't see da value of life because his ain't worth much. So a young, male dyin' is just another story to be told on dem number blocks.

See amerikkka wants to change but deep down they don't won't and need these type of dudes to exist. Homes are destroyed and yet expected to flourish in this amerikkkan dream bull—. Nah, for many of us we are born into a f— amerikkkan nightmare.[3]

It's a long-running nightmare in Newark. The nightmare continues on the streets of Oakland.

TRAPPED ON THE TRACK

The darkest place in Oakland is "the track." Why do we call it that? At a horse track, once the horses start moving, they never stand still. They run around in an endless circle. Well, in the 'hood we don't have horses. We have broken human beings who trudge sad-eyed, back and forth, mentally chained to a single block. They wear high heels, short skirts, bikinis, the provocative, and the next to nothing. To stop walking might mean an arrest for loitering or prostitution. To move too slowly might get the attention of a pimp in a car speeding by who might holler, "Shake yo, break yo self, ho!" (translated: "Step up your efforts to attract customers").

Pimps sometimes use the steps of a church building the way that the old-time slave trader would have used an auction block. In the flesh trade, the precious human body goes to the highest bidder. Sometimes church members have to walk past the spectacle to get inside to worship Jesus. Keep reading. It gets deeper.

There is a cold wind rushing through the streets of Oakland tonight. You'd best zip up your windbreaker. See that girl walking in the tight miniskirt and the stiletto heels marching with her head down? If you stare too long, she'll look in the opposite direction, but try to get a glimpse of her face before she does. How old does she look to you? Fourteen? Fifteen? Sixteen at the oldest? Who is she? Where did she come from? Where are her parents? How did she get in this situation?

Maybe she was kidnapped. Perhaps a car rolled up to her one day while she was strolling through the mall parking lot. Three men jumped out. One opened the trunk, the other two picked her up and threw her into the trunk. She pounded on the hood as her helpless body jumped up and down like a ping pong ball in the darkness. Two hours later, the trunk opened. Daylight blinded her. As she adjusted her eyes to the sun, she saw that one of the men had a sawed-off shotgun aimed at her brow. "Climb out," he growled. They marched her into a hotel room. For the next eight hours, men—all total strangers—moved in and out of the room. They took turns using her body. Some snapped pictures as souvenirs. Her screams eventually turned to whimpers. When morning light shone through the window, the one with the shotgun showed her pictures he had taken from her wallet. He said he knew where she lived. He had photos of her two sisters and said that if she didn't cooperate, her sisters could easily take her place. And that's how she ended up on that desolate street, walking around in a miniskirt on a chilly Bay Area night.

Many girls (and boys) who end up here were in foster care. They were removed from their homes because of parental neglect or abuse. Perhaps mom got arrested, and with no one to take care of the babies, the state of California had to assume responsibility. The tales of sexual abuse in many foster homes are widespread. As a child is passed from home to home, they often come into contact with predators, pedophiles who take advantage of their vulnerability.

Pimps often roost outside of group homes where foster children are housed. The exploiter might court her like a boyfriend. He may buy her nice things, get her hair styled, or get her nails done. Then comes the day he tells her she must requite his kindness. She has no father to protect her; he's in prison. If she goes missing, who will look diligently for her? She is officially his property. She is given a set of rules that must be obeyed. The least infraction might cause him to bring the pimp hand down (translated: he will torture her). The pimp keeps her under control by a mixture of fear, awe, and a twisted sense of loyalty. He must brainwash her into believing he is the omnipotent god of the streets. The younger she is, the more valuable. The pimp pockets thousands each week from her hide. Her longevity in what is known as the "Life" is not long. I remember looking into the eyes of a sexually exploited young woman whose face had been chopped up by a razor blade. Who did it? A sadistic john? A pimp unsatisfied with her earnings?

Once pimpdom was the domain of mysterious characters who operated with rules and codes. They drove flashy cars and dressed in flamboyant clothes. These new pimps are the spawn of the hip-hop game. They wear sneakers, hence the derogatory term "tennis shoe pimps."

Look anywhere human trafficking takes place, and you'll find that it grows in poverty like mold spores in a petri dish. The stress of hunger, homelessness, broken homes, the availability of drugs, the traumatic aftermath of random violence, and the lack of mental health services exacerbate the vulnerable situations where children might find themselves. Why would a child submit to the horrors of human trafficking? How could she allow a pimp to take advantage of her? Often because she faced hell in her home. Perhaps she had state-approved foster parents who sexually abused her and saw her as little more than a check. At least the pimp pretends to love her and to some extent will protect her. She's an investment, a human ATM. Her life span will not be long. Who will remember her when she is gone?

HOW CAN WE RESIST?

Look into the eyes of the homeless person laid out on the sidewalk munching spoiled fruit. Look at the prisoner doing life clutching the iron bars. Look at the thirty-year-old woman who appears to be seventy as she does circuits around the track. What do they all have in common? Once they were all seven years old.

It's easiest to reach a human being before development has ceased. Where I come from, the older folks have a saying that relates to this: "Bend the tree while it is still green." Be a presence in the life of a child while their mental framework and emotional capacity are still being forged. Does your church have an outreach to the children in a four-block radius of your building? Are you partnering with the local public school to see what services your church or ministry might provide? Are you involved in any kind of mentoring program?

Pimps and gang leaders hunt for preteen children to groom. Children are intensely loyal and obey without question. A child who joins a gang at twelve may still be a member at age sixty. Why don't you target these same children for the kingdom of God?

Too often, we have grown comfortable within the walls of the church, content to nurture our own and the children who have come of age in our religious social circles. We're apathetic to the needs of unchurched, unloved children who live in the shadows of our church buildings.

But that's all dead now. We've repented before God of our laziness concerning his call to rescue our fellow humanity. We're throwing dirt on apathy and laziness. As I said, this is the day of the resistance, and we'll spark this revolution by embracing the children.

Heal the children. To heal our children, we first must tell some uncomfortable truths within the church. Sermons about subjects like abuse and molestation must be preached. Hurting people must be the recipients of ministry. Broken families, particularly the curse of fatherlessness, cannot be met with silence. We have to move beyond the walls of our churches to communities that need healing and children who need to be embraced.

Nicia De'Lovely is a Bay Area poet and an advocate for sexually abused and commercially exploited children. In an interview for this book, she said,

> There are kids right now who are being sex trafficked right out of the church house! There are adults living with trauma in church. They stay there because they can't cope with the reality, and if they leave, they'll hurt themselves. Why are certain subjects off-limits?
>
> If we were to take away the church ceilings and walls that shelter our congregations, would we still be able to call what was left a church? I mean, take away the pews and the carpet; now it's just the streets and the people. Would the believers be living in their calling? If you can picture this scenario, you'll agree that there are no walls to hide behind in the world.
>
> Jesus was letting people touch his robe. He was touching people with leprosy. People were drawn to his nature as well as the way he nurtured people. He was outside with the people.
>
> Today, leaders are hidden inside the safety of buildings. They are hiding from the very people they are supposed to

be touching. Preacher, this is your obligation. Jesus would be pissed.[4]

Role models needed. Many inner-city churches have become commuter churches. That's not necessarily a bad thing. Not only do these churches have financial resources to share with the 'hood, but they also have human capital. You have doctors, lawyers, school teachers, successful entrepreneurs, and college students driving from the suburbs into the 'hood to worship. What an incredible pool of role models in a 'hood destabilized by the vast number of incarcerated adults!

Years ago I worked as a case manager for a continuation high school for inner-city kids who hadn't made it in a traditional school. I was given the responsibility of teaching a skills class. So, one day I invited a friend who had retired from UPS to come to talk about his professional life. I'll never forget how one young man's jaw dropped as he said, "You retired from UPS!" My friend might as well have been a former UN ambassador as far as this young fellow was concerned. The youth was blown away that my friend had possessed the steadfastness to hold on to his job, a good job, until retirement. So, no, you don't have to have a six-figure job to be a role model. Most adults have something to model for urban youth.

Be a mentor. Jaime Taylor is the executive director of Urban Mentors, a grassroots organization that could be a national model for faith-based organizations who reach out to inner-city children. Urban Mentors fills the void of belonging that negative 'hood figures tend to exploit. There are weekly meetings where singing, performance art, and arts and crafts are embraced.

There is prayer. Scriptures are read. The youth do community-building exercises like visiting senior citizens in retirement homes. They go on trips to rural areas far from the 'hood. The organization provides food and clothing to struggling parents. I call it an organization, but it is more like a structured band of loving adults and children who share together and bond around positive things.

Jaime and her staff wrap their arms around youth who need Jesus and loving adults to reveal a better way. You can do the same thing. Do urban young people come to Sunday school at your church? Go door-to-door in a campaign to invite them. Invite them to your Vacation Bible School in the summer. Start an Awana Youth Ministry or a Good News Club where kids can hear the gospel. Make sure to provide some refreshments at the end.

Protect the youth in your ministry. Nicia De'Lovely said, "Churches need formal training from certified professionals on the subject of sexual molestation and abuse. Bring experts in the field of human trafficking to the church so that churches can learn how to protect their children. The local church needs training for awareness, prevention, and healing. We need training to deal with all forms of post-traumatic stress disorder."[5]

I would go further. Adults who work with children need to have a certified background check. When reaching out to children, everything possible should be done to ensure their safety.

My mother's example. When I was a child, my mother, the late Claudette Davis Williams, became deeply immersed in Child Evangelism Fellowship. Her ministry began in our living room. Once a week Mama would gather my friends and teach us a Bible story. She was a master at telling flannelgraph stories. She would cut out figures of Bible characters and pin them on a cloth board. Back in the 1970s, that was state-of-the-art technology. We would sit there transfixed, teleported back to 500 BC. You could almost smell the sheep and hear them walking across the carpet. We were taught Bible choruses, which we sang completely off key but with gusto. At the end of the hour, there would be cookies and punch.

This Bible study grew to the point that the children could no longer fit inside the living room. From there, it was moved to our church. Dozens of kids would come to hear about Jesus. The group continued to grow. My mother added a second day on the other side of town in the Westside Community Center. Mama brought a van so she could carry kids back and forth. There was Vacation Bible Study in the summer.

My mother was a public high school teacher who loved fine clothes, but she grew up in poverty and part of that never left her. It was her joy to take kids from the most economically distressed areas of the city to summer camp. I can still remember jogging behind Mama up the stairs of the housing projects to visit parents who had not signed permission slips.

She filled the church bus and took kids to Upstate New York and Maryland for summer camp. Mama enrolled us in the Bible Memory Association program in which we learned Scripture passages that would stay with us for decades. Even today, people contact me on social media to tell me of the impact her ministry had on their lives.

My mother was a woman who prayerfully submitted to the will of God. In her seasons of prayer, the Lord gave her visionary ideas that would reroute the destiny of many young people in our city. From her, I learned that with God nothing is impossible. We didn't use the word *resistance* back then, but *apathy* was not in her dictionary. Nothing connected to ministry was half-way done or slipshod. She was in with both high heels. I didn't know it then, but she was indoctrinating her son to the resistance.

Helping from afar. I have friends who are burdened for people groups they will probably never visit—people in the Himalayas, China, or East Africa. They send money to Bible societies and mission groups who are on the front lines doing the real work in those places. They send money to relief organizations they have thoroughly investigated. You can do the same thing. However, be wise about your giving. Make sure that your dollars are going where they're supposed to. Be sure to pick up a copy of *Toxic Charity: How Churches and Charities Hurt Those They Help and How to Reverse It*, by Robert Lupton.

In the streets of Oakland, I have met some remarkable servants of humanity. I have broken bread with people who negotiate conflicts headed for bloodshed. I've met people who help children escape human trafficking. I have met Bible-believing preachers with the unique gift to reach people in the most desperate situations with the gospel of hope. Besides their demonstrated sincerity, they often have one thing in common: they are broke. They operate in situations where a fifty-dollar bill could make a difference. With a supermarket gift card, they can stop a kid from committing a crime in order to buy groceries for the family. A hundred dollars might keep some family's lights on. The money you spend on a movie and popcorn might be able to stop a bullet better than a Kevlar vest.

Who is doing the real work, the boots-on-the-ground work, within a two-hundred-mile radius of your front door? Do some research. One of the ministries you come across undoubtedly could use your check. Will you share?

HOMEWORK

- Remember the wet little child lying in his blankets on Powell Street? Capture him in your imagination. Write a letter to him. Write a prayer for him.
- Write an essay while the thoughts and emotions are still fresh in your mind. Finish with a prayer for him and children like him.

GENTRIFICATION

*What Happens When There's No
Direction Home?*

T he term *gentrification* was first coined by Ruth Glass, an English sociologist. It is the process whereby people with significant income identify a poor neighborhood they consider the hip, chic place to live. Often it is close to high-end employment or a blossoming nightlife scene. Causa Justa: Just Cause, a community-based tenants'-rights organization established in Oakland, says, "The profit-driven race and class remake of urban, working-class communities of color that have suffered from a history of divestment and abandonment—is evident all over urban centers in the US, where longtime communities are being pushed out of their homes."[1]

I recall the first time I became acquainted with the word *gentrification*. In the mid-1980s I was living in Harlem, New York, and was walking down West 125th Street when someone handed me a faded flier inviting me to the showing of a documentary regarding the rumored impending mass removal of black people from Harlem. It wasn't hard to understand how this could become a reality. It had a lot to do with logistics.

Harlem sits like a crown at the top of the borough of Manhattan. The financial center of the entire world was located downtown from the world's most famous ghetto. Each morning, New York City's white-collar citizens slogged their way across the other four boroughs and squeezed together in filthy, sweaty cattle-car subways to get to Manhattan. Why would a well-to-do person want to commute from Queens in Harlem when they could hop on the bus and zip down to work in a matter of fifteen minutes?

The documentary showed the nuts and bolts of how this would all happen. I remember little of the movie, but I do recall the raucous discussion that broke out as the credits rolled. The Q&A devolved into a near riot, with the moderator being run over with people shouting things like "Over my dead body!" Afterward, the front doors opened to the public school auditorium, allowing the storm to move out into the streets. By the next day the issue was forgotten, at least in my mind. I put the whole thing down to fear-mongering. Harlem was black. Harlem was affordable. Harlem was ours and would always be ours.

Back in the 1980s, my favorite sweatshirt had the words "Harlem: Capital of the Black Man's World" emblazoned on the front. I was wearing that shirt on the night that the impresario at the Barry Island Soul Festival in Wales introduced me. I can still hear his words thunder, "And now from Harlem, New York, the Incredible Mr. Freeze!" and I launched into my hip-hop single "Back to the Scene of the Crime."[2]

No, I wasn't really from Harlem. That is to say, I wasn't born there. I was living there in the 1980s, the darkest time in Harlem's history, the days when the crack menace had seized the city by the throat, and crack rocks and bullets were falling from a blood-red sky.

I was born on the other side of the metropolis, in Brooklyn, a bridge and thirty miles away. However, Harlem has been the spiritual and cultural center of the Africa diaspora for more than a century. I used to take my meals at a greasy-spoon restaurant on Lenox Avenue that had a black and white portrait on the wall of Harlem Renaissance poet Langston Hughes. Below, it said, "Langton Hughes Used to Eat Here." In Harlem, I walked streets that were home to Duke Ellington, Billie Holiday, Marcus Garvey, and Malcolm X. I stopped to listen to black nationalist preachers and Pentecostal evangelists as they vied for my heart and soul. Harlem was a big African village where grits and hot links, Jamaica beef patties, and the Senegalese specialty thiéboudienne delighted the palate.

Of course, Harlem was not paradise. It was an impoverished place where far too many people struggled to just get by. I know because I was one of them. Still, Harlem had soul, an earthiness. I remember the cinnamon- and mocha-colored faces of the people I called my neighbors. I remember nodding at a cabal of senior citizens on my way to work as they sold shots of unlicensed liquor and played cards. The saying of the neighborhood, which became 'hood scripture, was "Don't knock the hustle."

Make no mistake about it. When I lived in Harlem, it was segregated. I worked in downtown Manhattan, the multiracial business hub of the world. At the end of a shift, a mixed multitude crowded into the subway. The street numbers rose higher as we traveled north. Times Square is located at 42nd Street. By the time we reached 110th Street, the Harlem border, most often no white

45

people remained on the subway. Soul great Bobby Womack had a hit song called "Across 110th Street," which was the soundtrack to the movie of the same name.

In 1984, Joe Morton starred in the film *Brother from Another Planet*. It was the story of a space alien pursued by extraterrestrial police. At one point the alien, who lands in Harlem, has assumed the form of a black man and is riding the subway. A magician sitting across from him asks, "Hey, do you want me to make all of the white people disappear?"[3] If you were from New York City, you were already in on the joke. The next stop was West 110th Street, and of course every soul on the train was black by that time.

Most black people didn't choose Harlem as home because it was an enclave of black culture or because it was a place of respite from overt racism. They chose the world beyond 110th Street because the rent was affordable. Black Harlem had been there for a hundred years, and back in the mid- to late 1980s, few could envision the day when it would change.

WHERE HAS MY HOME GONE?

I had the opportunity to visit the East Coast during summer 2017. I knew that I couldn't go home without visiting Harlem. I took the 8th Avenue subway from Penn Station straight back to my old 'hood. My heart beat furiously. I wondered if I'd run into any of the people I used to know. The train stopped at West 116th Street. Suspense pushed on me. I departed the train car and climbed up the steep steps as fast as my legs could carry me.

Minutes later I was blinded by the sunlight. A new prosperity had come to Harlem. An outdoor beer garden had sprung up where once there was just an empty lot strewn with broken glass and crack vials. Anglo folks laughed and smiled as a few remaining people from the 'hood walked by slowly, staring. A young blond woman who looked like she was on summer break from Cornel University stood on one corner selling fresh bagels. A group of well-heeled white women toting bags from Nordstrom and Macy's strutted by me. I walked to the corner where the senior citizens used to play cards, tell jokes, and sell an occasional illegitimate sip to the locals. Gone. I stopped at a coffee shop just a few blocks away to get my bearings. In the middle of Harlem, tea was being sold for five dollars a cup!

Change is inevitable. After all, Harlem was not always a black community. At the turn of the twentieth century, a collapse in the real estate market in Harlem forced wealthy landlords to break housing covenants and—for the first time—rent to blacks. First, one block turned shade and then another, and before long the Harlem I knew appeared.

Gentrification struck Harlem for many reasons. That part of New York is lined with beautiful brownstone mansions, many of which were cut up into rooms and apartments to house poor and working-class people. These stately walk-up buildings would have been worth a princely sum had they not been located in areas known for crime and blight. Most New Yorkers have to travel from the outer boroughs to get to Manhattan. Blight and a soaring crime rate kept Harlem segregated. And then the violent crime rate all over America fell dramatically. Neighborhoods that would have once been off-limits were made safe again through aggressive policing. Did these changes come for the benefit of the people who had lived in Harlem for decades, or were they for the sake of a new clientele, people with the money to revamp the brownstones and remake the community?

While change is inevitable, it's not always easy. One could sense an animosity in the air, a tension between those who had been able to hang on and those who had come uptown to take advantage of the new frontier. I watched as frowns, furtive side glances, smirks, and downcast faces beheld the fall of Harlem. Everyone I had known was gone. The bodegas, Italian ice emporiums, fish-and-chips houses, and walk-up Chinese food restaurants with bullet-proof glass partitions—all gone.

BUY OUT THE MISSION

The tech boom of the twenty-first century brought an incredible infusion of prosperity to the San Francisco Bay Area. Tech giants like Yahoo!, Facebook, Google, and others relocated to this relatively small, already densely populated space. Who could blame the young tech workers for wanting to live here? The weather is great year-round. The area is beautiful—from the Pacific Ocean to the rolling hills that spread over the horizon. San Francisco is one of the top tourist destinations in the world. It boasts renowned restaurants and legendary nightlife.

The problem is that San Francisco does not have large swaths of uninhabited land to convert into housing tracts. Where would these well-heeled newcomers live?

The Mission District was one of the first places to experience gentrification. Traditionally a Latino enclave, the Mission was home to bakeries where bolillos, buñuelos, and truffle cakes were baked and sold. Vendors marched up and down the street selling homemade onion rings and sweet corn. On Saturday afternoons, families who had been living in the community for generations walked together to St. James Catholic Church at Guerrero and 23rd Street for Mass.

In a city where rents have been relatively expensive for a long time, poor people could afford the rent in the Mission District. The tech explosion changed that. Landlords in the Mission District realized there was a new clientele who could pay three or four times the amount of rent than the people who had lived in the area for generations. The Mission began to change around 2005 as landlords took advantage of this new windfall. Builders scooped up dilapidated properties, destroyed them, and built high-end condominiums. Dimly lit bars where locals once spun on the floor to music from El Salvador, Chile, and Mexico are now soulless hipster hangouts where conversations center on existentialism or the best beaches in Saint-Tropez. Of course, among all of the laughter and joy, there are consequences that are served mostly to the poor and lower-middle class who will be displaced by spiraling rent or priced out by the brand-new condos on their block, which were not created with them in mind.

The market forces that brought the tech workers to the Mission are like tornadoes that not only blow down houses but shift landscapes. San Francisco is now one of the most expensive cities on the North American continent. People who once lived in upper-middle-class neighborhoods often find themselves displaced as well. Where will they live? If they want to continue to live in the Bay Area, they will move to poor communities historically populated by people of color.

Places like South Berkeley and Oakland, which lie in San Francisco's shadows, were next in line to fall. Professionals who work in San Francisco began to note that West Oakland, a black community dotted with Victorian mansions and brimming with history, is located only fifteen minutes from downtown San Francisco.

THE DARKEST SIDE OF GENTRIFICATION

One single mom's rent nearly doubled when the landlord found out that San Francisco tech workers were both willing and happy to relocate to Oakland and pay an exorbitant sum for housing in a building once labeled a tenement. For the tech workers, it was affordable rent in the most expensive place to live in America. It was also an easy commute.

For the single mother, things were a bit more complicated. She had three children. She had to purchase bus fare, cereal, and school clothes. She was barely scraping by on her minimum-wage job at a local fast-food restaurant. Where would she and her children go if they lost this one-bedroom apartment?

The woman pleaded with the landlord not to raise the rent so high, appealing to his sense of humanity. He was unyielding, threatening to kick her and her children into the streets. Finally, he offered a compromise. Now, several times a month, she must follow him into a dark, unlit stairwell where she will service him sexually in order to offset the portion of the rent that is beyond her means to pay.

Yes, this young mother is ashamed. She loathes even the scent of him. Her sense of self-esteem sinks every time he touches her hand and leads her toward the shadows. However, she sees no other options. This is what must be done to keep her family together. She just prays that her children do not find out. They would not understand.

THE AFTERMATH

In the Bay Area, San Francisco and Oakland are employment hubs. People who have been priced out of the area have been forced over the hills into faraway cities where the cost of living is less of a cross to bear on the shoulders of the human soul. Often, their new homes are in hardscrabble locales where the climate is desert-like in the summer months.

If the displaced have been fortunate to hold on to their jobs, they make the morning commute back to the Bay. It can take two hours in brutal bumper-to-bumper traffic or through dense fog. Teachers, firefighters, bus drivers, and police join the parade of cars and trucks, only to pay exorbitant parking fees for the next eight hours.

On Sundays, displaced worshipers sometimes tire of making the journey back to San Francisco or Oakland for the sixth day in the span of a week. Many eventually relinquish their memberships in the churches that have been their spiritual homes for generations. Neighborhoods that once housed prominent African American churches have now completely priced the members out of the communities.

Gentrification separates families, something that even segregation was unable to do. At least segregation allowed us to live in the same geographical areas: grandmother and grandson might live in the same public housing project. Gentrification disperses the family as rents and mortgages dictate where people of limited income may live.

Inner-city communities offer many benefits to people who are financially limited. Public transportation in cities like San Francisco makes it possible to get around without owning an automobile. There is access to medical care. Transport services help the sick and the elderly get to their appointments. San Francisco has free legal services that protect the poor from vampire landlords. Churches and nonprofit centers offer free food.

Imagine removing access to all of those benefits. There they are, a family of five living in a broken-down trailer on a back street in a California town with none of San Francisco's great resources. The reality is stark and ugly, but there is more.

HOMELESSNESS: GENTRIFICATION'S COUSIN

I was sitting in a coffee shop preparing to get started on this manuscript one afternoon when I was interrupted. A woman cleared her throat, leaned down to where I was seated, and said, "Hi, Rev. Harry! You don't remember me, do you?"

I squinted and peered deeply into her eyes. I looked at the shape of her nose, her hair. I didn't recognize her. And then she said her name. I recognized it. Oddly enough, the name and figure in front of me didn't match. They seemed to belong to two different people. She filled in the blank: "I'm homeless."

How could that have been possible? I had been invited to her suburban home years earlier for a succulent, Sunday dinner with some other folks. She was educated. She presented well.

"I'm living in my car," she said. I believed her. Who would lie about a thing like that? Perhaps I could help her. We exchanged phone numbers.

The price of housing has skyrocketed in the San Francisco Bay Area. That is not the only figure that has inflated. By some estimates, the homeless population has mushroomed 25 percent within the past two years! The inflated cost of housing is literally driving people onto the streets. Scores of tent cities exist between freeways in the downtown area, even in front of churches.

Homeless men and women in raincoats and backpacks wait out their days in the city libraries. They ride the buses and trains back and forth. They set up tents behind gas stations. They live in abandoned buildings. Homeless shelters in the area where I live are overflowing. People walk the streets day and night, folks who once had places to live but were displaced. Gentrification has turned low-income 'hoods into high-income paradises.

In 2008, at the height of the Great Recession, Oakland was torn apart by foreclosures. It turns out that many people had bought houses with generous terms extended to them by lending institutions. At some point, the terms allowed for these mortgages to spike outrageously. All over lower-income communities, homes were seized and boarded up by banks. Corporate investors grabbed up an unholy 42 percent of homes lost to foreclosure. Ninety-three percent of these houses were in the Oakland flatlands, homes largely occupied by people of color.

May I predict the future for you? Whole swaths of urban Oakland are now owned by corporate raiders and wealth industries, which exist to make profits. Oakland's pockets of poverty exist in the middle of the most expensive real estate in North America. Eventually, these corporations will transform those 'hoods into hip, desirable communities with bike lanes, cappuccino bars, and wine-tasting venues.

CONFRONTING THE BEAST

In the Gospels we find an account of a man who follows Jesus down the road declaring, "I will follow you wherever you go."

Jesus, who was never known to water down the cost of discipleship, said to him, "Foxes have dens and birds have nests, but the Son of Man has no place to lay his head" (Luke 9:57-58).

Jesus challenged the would-be follower with an extreme scenario, the prospect of homelessness, to drift and not to rest, to endure the storms of life without sanctuary. Today, as in the first century, to live without stable housing is a loathsome burden. However, to be fair, Jesus was proposing the concept to a grown, able-bodied man. Most people affected by gentrification and homelessness in America are women and children.

When Jesus looked at multitudes of people and discerned that they were hungry, he fed them. When they were sick, he healed them. In the early church, deacons were set aside to care for the needs of widows. Discerning those needs and meeting them were simple to strategize. Fast forward to the civil rights movement. It was relatively easy to look at a segregated lunch counter and realize that force was needed for integration to occur. Gentrification is not so easy to fix. It's a systemic evil that has a number of tentacles protruding from it. Decades before the first poor person is displaced, people sit in back rooms or on golf carts at the country club planning how whole communities will be overturned. Political policy decisions, banking institution decisions, market forces, uninformed communities, and a host of other things fuel the steamroller called gentrification. At the end of the day, conversations held far from the 'hood decide who gets to live inside and who doesn't.

WHAT CAN BE DONE?

What can we do about gentrification?

Expand your theology. Many believers will not fight to save their own communities because they don't see it as primary to their spiritual mission. They assume that if a topic is not directly connected to soul salvation or holiness, it should not be the focus of a church's energy. Ironically, many churches with this belief system have had the entire community around them gentrified while they did nothing. Christian theology holds in tension the balance between the heretofore and the hereafter. The prophet Amos rails, "Let justice roll on like a river, righteousness like a never-failing stream" (Amos 5:24). Later, Jesus tells Nicodemus, "You should not be surprised at my saying, 'You must be born again'" (John 3:7). God cares about the whole person. God wants to be connected to us in a personal relationship. God also wants us to have safe, affordable housing. It's not either-or. It is both-and.

Understand how public policy works. Gentrification does not just happen. It is driven by market forces, zoning ordinances, and political policy. It's like a slow-moving steamroller at the top of a hill. It takes a while to get in motion, but once it starts moving, it crushes everything in its path and is almost impossible to stop. Therefore, we need to know the warning signs. We need to attend city council meetings, invite our local officials out for tea, and discover their stances. We must become educated voters and register others to vote. People have died for the right to vote in America because a vote represents a voice heard. Our vote is powerful. We can learn how public policy is crafted, how laws are made, and how voting measures find their way to the polls.

Empower others. In Oakland the slogan "Power to the people" has been in existence since the sixties. When a community is slated for gentrification, the people who live there stand to lose everything. We can face that battle two different ways. We can be a savior who rides in on a white horse to save the commoners, or we can bring to the table the people most affected, allow them to advocate for themselves, and empower them to lead the struggle.

Help people before they become homeless. Sometimes people are evicted over small amounts of rent and then it is hard for them to get another place to live with an eviction on their record. In some cities there are nonprofit organizations, even churches, who will help people put that sum of money together. It's much easier to help someone pay a few months back rent in a somewhat affordable apartment building than to help them gather two months' worth of deposit money and the first month's rent.

Tent city ministry. Where do people go after eviction? Sometimes they board a train back to the welcoming arms of relatives in another state. Some sleep on a friend's couch or in homeless shelters. In states like California, where the weather tends to be milder, folks band together beneath freeways or in public parks to create urban living spaces reminiscent of Bangladesh in the 1970s. There are old tires, food scraps, stray dogs, and plenty of rats racing around a sea of multicolored tents. There are inadequate bathing facilities, and food and drinking water are at a premium in the average tent city. What a marvelous place and opportunity to fulfill the Great Commission! Bring water. Bring blankets. Bring gently used clothing. Bring socks. Bring food. You might conduct a prayer service. Either way, the folks trapped in these American hells will be touched by the hand of Jesus when you show up with the life-sustaining supplies they need.

Understand that gentrification is a spiritual stronghold. Anything that displaces the children, the elderly, and the disabled from their homes is unholy. The apostle Paul says,

> Our struggle is not against flesh and blood, but against the rulers, against the authorities, against the powers of this dark world and against the spiritual forces of evil in the heavenly realms. Therefore put on the full armor of God, so that when the day of evil comes, you may be able to stand your ground, and after you have done everything, to stand. (Ephesians 6:12-13)

ADDRESSING ISSUES OF POVERTY AND INEQUALITY

In my first semester in seminary, a professor gave us a rather challenging assignment. We were to outline a passage of Scripture and then exegete it using all of the resource materials at our disposal. I chose Matthew 25.

As I pored through abstracts, Bible dictionaries, and commentaries I was surprised at how the meaning of Jesus' words varied from scholar to scholar. A large number of great thinkers throughout history surmised that Jesus' commands to care for the hungry, the naked, and imprisoned were metaphorical. They said that Jesus meant we were to feed those hungry for the Word. We were to clothe those naked to spiritual attack because they lacked the armor of God. Others believed that Jesus called us to visit those imprisoned by sin. Well, as far as I am concerned, you have to be a theological contortionist to draw those conclusions. And while

I was working on that assignment something happened that made it clear to me.

Looking for a respite from our studies, several of my fellow seminarians proposed going to a movie on a Saturday afternoon. I can't remember what we saw, but I do remember what I saw when we came out of the theater. A mother walking down the street with her children saw the big barrel of popcorn we had and said, "My son is hungry. Can he have that popcorn?"

It took me back a bit. We handed her the popcorn. She was homeless. They'd been evicted and were living in her car. There was no food. I believed that because the kids were scarfing down the popcorn like they hadn't eaten in a week. The kids were ragged, their shoes were run down, and their eyes were hollow from malnutrition.

Poor students of God's Word that we were, we dug deep and blessed her with what money we had in our pockets, which wasn't much. She thanked us graciously and then walked away with her kids. And I went back to the seminary library to work on the assignment. As I meditated on this Scripture in the light of my encounter with that homeless family, it was as though I had never read it before or heard it preached in context from the pulpit. Jesus' three-dimensional image of Judgment Day is one of the most riveting teachings of his entire ministry. Especially the exchange between the Son of Man and the startled people now labeled "goats." Jesus said,

> Then [the King] will say to those on his left, "Depart from me, you who are cursed, into the eternal fire prepared for the devil and his angels. For I was hungry and you gave me

nothing to eat, I was thirsty and you gave me nothing to drink, I was a stranger and you did not invite me in, I needed clothes and you did not clothe me, I was sick and in prison and you did not look after me."

They also will answer, "Lord, when did we see you hungry or thirsty or a stranger or needing clothes or sick or in prison, and did not help you?"

He will reply, "Truly I tell you, whatever you did not do for one of the least of these, you did not do for me."

Then they will go away to eternal punishment, but the righteous to eternal life. (Matthew 25:41-46)

Was Jesus speaking about the needs they'd ignored in some nebulous, metaphorical sense? Hardly. Jesus lived in a nation stripped of its sovereignty and wealth by the Roman Empire. More than likely, Jesus knew friends who were evicted from farms that had been in their families for generations due to crushing tax debt. The political situation reduced people to beggars and prostitutes. Because of his great love for humanity, the inequity and brutal poverty unleashed on the people branded itself on his soul. Is it any wonder that he would send people to eternal punishment for ignoring the needs of the poor?

What if Jesus had been born in the twenty-first century instead of the first? This portion of Scripture might have another paragraph or two tacked on. In the addendum, Jesus might have something to say about our responses to miseducated children, police brutality, mass incarceration, and the unbridled greed that feeds gentrification. Inequality in America is not a simple matter of sending a bread truck and used clothing to the poor. Poverty is maintained by systems and policies. Lazy religion says, "God doesn't mean that every believer fits in this Scripture. It's only for people with a special calling." The resistance says, "Oh God, help us all because we are guilty. We repent. Now tell us where to start!"

HOMEWORK

- Google the word *gentrification* next to your hometown's name. See what comes up. Google *gentrification* with the name of the nearest major city to your residence. What did you find?

- If gentrification is not confronted, what happens to the poor children and the widows? What can you do? Write an essay.

CROSSING CULTURES

Understanding the World of Urban Ministry

I have been a huge *Star Trek* fan since Leonard Nimoy fanned out his fingers and said, "Live long and prosper." The amazing imagination of the show's creator, Gene Roddenberry, was evident in the original *Star Trek* version of space travel.

When the troops on the starship *USS Enterprise* wanted to descend to a planet beneath them, they stood on a special platform on the spacecraft, and their atoms were disassembled and then reassembled on the planet's surface. This was called "beaming down." Once they were on the planet, they faced the often significantly different natives there.

Urban ministry works the same way. Whether you are called to share the gospel outside the ragged front door of a crack house in the 'hood or with a new neighbor who just moved to town from another state, you are going to have to take some drastic steps to fit into their world, to understand them. That person may share your skin color and hair texture, but their view of life has been shaped by a reality different from yours. Starship cadet, imagine how different your view of life might be from someone of another culture.

The basic laws of communication work like this: a thought forms in your mind and you encode it into words; you translate your thoughts into words. The words are never exactly the same as your original thoughts. You share your words based on the breadth of your vocabulary, your command of language, and your worldview, which is based on your culture, your home, your parents, your faith tradition, and so on. Finally, the words land on the other person's eardrums. The people receiving your communication must decode what you say through their worldview, life experiences, family of origin, and so on. What you think and say is going to be different from what they hear. The height of hubris is to say, "Why don't they get it?"

Years ago, a pastor came to town from a distant city. He said that God had sent him to minister in a black and Latino community I knew intimately. Five minutes into our initial conversation, I realized that if this preacher was going to be successful in leading the resistance, he would need some powerful cultural advice.

He would need the benefit of insights that I had gathered over a lifetime of being black in an urban context. I gave him a collection of books to read. I was always in his ear about decisions that would best serve him in his quest to bring hope to the 'hood.

He didn't listen.

He illustrated his sermons with stories about skiing and mountain climbing. He spoke on everything from redaction criticism to transubstantiation. In the midst of his lengthy ad-dresses, members of color would glance back and forth at each other, totally lost. What started off with a flurry of excitement ended in a desert of empty seats. His church folded, and the preacher left town never to be seen again. Like many members of the dominant culture, he assumed (perhaps subconsciously) that his viewpoint was the only correct one. That assumption failed him miserably.

YOUR WORLDVIEW

Your unique view of the world is formulated out of the social context you were born into. Your worldview was sketched by pastors, school teachers, parents, community, and a myriad of other people, things, and experiences. When we say that something is true, our belief is based on the hundreds of thousands of fragments of personal data that constitute our personal truth. The trouble begins when we insist that everyone sees the world through our lenses because our lenses are the only correct ones.

In the classic movie *The African Queen*, starring Humphrey Bogart and Katharine Hepburn, a missionary and his sister plant a church in a remote African village. As the film begins, a worship service is in progress. It looks like it's 150 degrees outside, and the missionary's sister is clothed in a dress that buttons at the neck, covers the arms, and falls to her button-up black shoes. She hops on the organ and begins playing a traditional American hymn. As she and her brother sing, the brothers and sisters of the village are encouraged to chime in. The thing is, they don't speak English. They yammer and holler off-key. The whole thing is just a mishmash of noise.

When the song is finished and the sermon is delivered, the pastor pats himself on the back for having preached God's Word to the natives. However, they don't know what he's talking about and more than likely think he's nuts. He can't speak their language. He knows nothing of their history. He doesn't know the first thing about them, nor does he feel that he needs that knowledge. He has been trained since he was in diapers to believe he and his culture are superior.

That school of ministry is alive and at work today. That is why an underground faith resistance is needed to provide an alternative approach.

I once attended a meeting of local pastors, each of a different ethnicity. When we walked into the room and took our seats, I noticed an unusual thing. The one white pastor present took the seat at the head of the table. He didn't question his right to take that seat; neither did the pastors of color. All seated at that table were programmed to believe that the white man was supposed to take that seat.

WHITE SUPREMACY

I remember the day I first realized that I was black. I was seven years old. By the time I arrived at ten years, I had a firm grip on what it meant to have brown skin and the struggles that my skin color would bring to me. I began to realize that there were upscale communities around me that were 100 percent white. Even the servants who worked there weren't black.

History class taught me that the vast majority of people who had done anything worth recording or remembering were white. I grew up in a world where Miss America was always white, and our psyches were so scarred that we didn't even question it. I grew up in a world where the astronauts and all of the presidents up till my time on earth had been white men. I grew up in a world where white people passed wealth down to their children through generations but few blacks could do the same. I was born into a world where the longevity rate for black men was much shorter than for white men. As a young person I found out what it was to be called "n—r" or "boy" or to have those things implied by teachers and authority figures even when they were not said. I had to learn how to fight racists who were so disquieted by my skin color that they felt the need to attack me physically.

According to psychologist Ken Hardy, it is not unusual for white people to be unaware of their whiteness until they are in college or graduate school. He said, "It is very hard to be white and not believe or have had it incorporated into your psyche that white is superior. White people are socialized not to talk about whiteness. White is a term that most white people never use. Most white people are rarely in a situation where they are a minority."[1]

Dr. Hardy went on to say, "We are all racially socialized. Race is a powerful organizing principle in our society. We can't even get our minds around how powerful it is. You can't devalue it. We live in a color-conscious society."

According to Dr. Hardy, most white people know little about how black people actually think. He says, "On the other hand, black people are experts on whiteness. We don't get the job without knowing what's important to white people. We *have* to know that. A black person cannot survive without that knowledge."[2]

BLACK IN A WORLD OF WHITE SUPREMACY

In actuality, race and color are fictive designations. There is no such thing as a black person or a white person. Those designations were created to justify the enslavement of black people and the genocide of the Native Americans. The term *white* was given to Europeans to enhance and perpetuate an "us and them" paradigm. When the English, Germans, Irish, and Italians landed in America, they did not see themselves as one people, "white" people. They saw themselves as English, German, Irish, and Italian. The idea of whiteness had to be created, and the impact of that fiction on people of color has been horrendous and long-lasting.

At the height of chattel slavery, it is said that a slaveowner from the West Indies was summoned to Virginia to demonstrate how rebellious slaves could be kept in line. His methods are discussed in what became known as the Willie Lynch papers.

According to Lynch,

These methods have worked on my modest plantation in the West Indies and it will work throughout the South. Take this simple little list of differences and think about them. On top of my list is "age" but it's there only because it starts with an "A." The second is "COLOR" or shade, there is intelligence, size, sex, size of plantations and status on plantations, attitude of owners, whether the slaves live in the valley, on a hill, East, West, North, South, have fine hair, course [*sic*] hair, or is tall or short. Now that you have a list of differences, I shall give you an outline of action, but before that, I shall assure you that distrust is stronger than trust and envy stronger than adulation, respect or admiration. The Black slaves after receiving this indoctrination shall carry on and will become self refueling and self generating for hundreds of years, maybe thousands. Don't forget you must pitch the old black Male vs. the young black Male, and the young black

Male against the old black Male. You must use the dark skin slaves vs. the light skin slaves, and the light skin slaves vs. the dark skin slaves. You must use the female vs. the male. And the male vs. the female. You must also have your white servants and overseers distrust all Blacks. It is necessary that your slaves trust and depend on us. They must love, respect and trust only us. Gentlemen, these kits are your keys to control. Use them. Have your wives and children use them, never miss an opportunity. If used intensely for one year, the slaves themselves will remain perpetually distrustful of each other.[3]

In her groundbreaking book *Post Traumatic Slave Syndrome*, author Joy DeGruy underscores the fact that the residue of slavery still exists in America. She writes,

One-hundred and eighty years of the Middle Passage, 246 years of slavery, rape and abuse; one hundred years of illusory freedom. Black codes, convict leasing, Jim Crow, all codified by our national institutions. Lynching, medical experimentation, grossly unequal treatment in almost every aspect of our society, brutality at the hands of those charged with protecting and serving. Being undesirable strangers in the only land we know. . . . [T]hree hundred and eighty-five years of physical, psychological and spiritual torture have left their mark.[4]

African Americans have experienced a legacy of trauma. DeGruy notes that multigenerational trauma, oppression, and institution racism continue today. I have to agree with her. I've seen it.

I was visiting with an Anglo faith leader who heads a ministry to black youth when one of the young men in his group said something that raised my eyebrows. He said, "You white people are so smart. How did you come to rule the world? How did you become so powerful?"

At first, I thought he was being sarcastic, but as the questions kept coming, I realized he was truly in awe of the white race and his faith leader, its representative. This being established in his mind, do you believe that he saw that white ministry leader as his equal or his lord? The history of hundreds of years is not wiped away with the quotation of some Bible verses. It has affected the way both whites and people of color view themselves in relation to one another.

Is there such a thing as white supremacy? Is white privilege a reality or a concept created by some disgruntled blacks? How can this poisonous bridge be dynamited?

RACE AND RELIGION

America is the story of Europeans seeking wealth and religious freedom and gaining both by slaughtering Native Americans and enslaving black people. It's not pretty, especially from the perspective of the people whose forbearers were ravaged. Race is a difficult thing to talk about, and as a result it is often not discussed in mixed company, even when circumstances demand that conversation.

Anglo missionaries who come to communities of color are urged not to be religious colonists but to journey beside the people they will serve. Listen to the people's stories. Hear their voices. Sit underneath the leadership of someone of color before you lead people of color. (That makes sense, doesn't it?) Understand that the people themselves are the best experts of their own experiences. Don't define them using the standards and perspectives of the world in which you grew up. Learn about their culture or cultures. Read. Attend cultural programs. In 1 Corinthians 9:22, Paul said, "I have become all things to all people so that by all possible means I might save some." Jaime Taylor followed that road.

BUILDING COMMUNITY IN THE INNER CITY

Jaime first came to Oakland as a short-term missionary through an organization called Mission Year. Her heart became attached to many of the people she met here. She never left. She started a girls' mentorship group in her living room, which grew into several different manifestations. It ended up becoming Urban Mentors, an organic, grassroots organization that offers one-on-one mentoring, group mentoring, community building, and family events in East Oakland. Many lives have been saved. Many destinies have been rerouted. Jaime has flaming red hair and brown freckles. She lives in the community where she ministers. She is a ball of boundless energy. Recently, I was able to catch up with her, and this is what she said about urban ministry over breakfast.

Entering into a community with the thought you're going to start something doesn't respect what's going on in your community. It doesn't acknowledge that there are people of faith and nonreligious groups who have been bleeding for that community for a long time and have something to teach you. As any outsider, you really don't know anything yet. Just because you read a couple of books and want to change the world and think that there are some poor people in the inner city who need Jesus, like, you're going to have to realize that they're going to have more to offer you than you'll have to offer them for the first ten years.

If you are planning to do urban ministry, come understanding you know nothing. I had run a shelter program. I had done some inner-city work. At twenty-three, I showed up here in Oakland thinking I had some experience under my belt and then realized I knew very little. Actually, staying in that place where you feel as though you know very little is always a good place to stay in ministry-wise.

Also remember, every person is different. Every family is different. Every neighborhood is different. I spent seventeen years in the black community in Oakland, but I know very little about the intricacies of what it means to be a Latino in Oakland. You can't assume that you are culturally competent because you worked with a certain population in a certain city. You're competent working with the people group you were with, not all people. Stay really humble and seek out the wisdom of those who were there before you.[5]

WHERE DO WE GO FROM HERE?

For years the church in America has stumbled over the issues of race and the color bar. It would be easy to continue to evade the subject or at best to mix a teaspoon of falsehood in with a cup of friendship. The real conversation about race and how we practice faith is long overdue. But it's not going to be easy.

The conversation about race is no coffee-time chitchat. Issues surrounding undocumented citizens and Muslim immigrants are razors that slice the body of Christ in half.

We bring racial attitudes to ministry especially as we do cross-cultural ministry. The actor Samuel L. Jackson does a commercial that always ends with the words "What's in your wallet?" I think we need to be free enough to ask each other, "What's in your baggage?"

White supremacy is deeply woven into the fabric of our church. It'll take a resistance movement—a people who refuse to be chained to the past—to wage it. It will take some truth telling. This will be one of the most uncomfortable parts of the journey, but the end result will be most rewarding.

HOMEWORK

- Write down the major points of this chapter. Gather friends and discuss these points. Next, discuss the points with a person whose background may be different from your own. Where do you find yourself in this discussion?
- What needs to change in order for healing to occur?
- What challenges present themselves in crosscultural ministry? Write a prayer to God concerning what you just read.

6 DEATH IN THE POT

The Story of Racism in America

I f the resistance is going to be successful, its soldiers will have to face a troublesome truth. The image of Jesus as a white man with flowing blond locks has had a profoundly negative impact on the African American community. For many, the image is the symbol of white supremacy just as the Statue of Liberty is the symbol of American freedom. Based largely on that image, many younger African American leaders reject the deity of Jesus and teach others to do the same. Throughout my life, people have told me it didn't really matter that Jesus Christ is usually depicted as a white man. How wrong they are. The falling away from the church by young African Americans is beginning to snowball. Many people of color equate the image of a white Jesus with the Christian faith itself.

THERE'S DEATH IN THE POT

In 2 Kings 4, the prophet Elijah commands his servant to create a pot of stew for the other prophets who have gathered with him at meal time. The servant goes out into a wooded area and returns with some vegetation. He tosses it into a pot, makes a stew, and serves it to the prophets. Stomachs are growling because Israel is experiencing famine. As the aroma rises from the bowls, the prophets discard with protocol and after hastily saying grace they begin slurping the food.

But something is wrong. It is inedible. One of the prophets looks at Elijah and tells him that there is death in the pot. What should have been nourishing and life-giving was an agent of destruction.

Elijah asks that an extra ingredient be added to the stew. Once the servant pours in flour, all is well, and they eat heartily.

Imagine if someone had kidnapped your grandfather, tied him up, and then dragged him into a building with a steeple on top. When Granddad looks up, there is a statue in front of him. Imagine the kidnapper told Granddad, "We'll whip you if you don't pray to this statue!" Granddad won't say the prayer. The kidnapper removes his sword from the sheath and forces Granddad's lips open with the sharp steel tip. He lets Granddad taste his own blood drawn by the sword. The kidnapper removes the sword from your grandfather's mouth and then implores Granddad to sound out the two-syllable name Jesus.

Granddad looks up at the blond-haired statue that so closely resembles the kidnapper and tries to approximate the name of the deity. Is it difficult to understand why one hundred years later some of Granddad's kin come across that story and reject the deity and the beliefs associated with Jesus?

Dear reader, like those prophets, many African Americans have sat down at the table and proclaimed that there is death in the pot of American Christianity. The words of abundant life and the respect for our common humanity have been mixed with a stew of slavery, racism, white privilege, misquotation, prejudice, and misrepresentations of Scripture. Add to that the image of Jesus

Christ most often held up as a Caucasian God, and you'll find the reason that many black people have abandoned the Christian faith.

Some blacks have adopted other religions; others have embraced atheism. A rejection of Christianity is growing among young blacks who refer to themselves as "conscious" or "woke." In future years, rejection of faith in Jesus as Lord is going to mushroom in the black community. True, only God through his Holy Spirit can reverse this trend, but if you and I are going to serve as colaborers in bringing the gospel to this shattered world, we must take an honest look inside the pot of our theology. Others have already taken off the lid and are peering inside.

FIVE-PERCENTERS

"The black man is god!" I can still hear the declaration reverberate through the halls of my high school as ex-Sunday school kids joyously announced their new revelation. Overnight, they'd been transformed. No longer would they answer to their "government" names. We were asked to call them by new titles or "righteous attributes," which were names like God Supreme, and Self-U-Savior. They wore knitted caps called "crowns" and greeted each other with the words "Peace, God." They spoke in coded language filled with numerology and scientific facts. Young men who had been unsuccessful in school memorized page after page of "Lessons," the sacred text of the Nation of the Five Percent.

The Nation of Gods and Earths was born in Harlem in 1964. Its founder was Clarence 13X, a disaffected member of the Nation of Islam who broke away to form his own sect. His original followers were disinherited black and Latino youth from the streets of the inner city. Clarence 13X taught that 85 percent of the people were deaf, dumb, and blind, lost to the knowledge of self. Ten percent knew the truth but concealed it. Five percent were the poor, righteous teachers whose mission was to civilize the lost. The founder taught his disciples that the black man was god.

Young black men seeking spirituality and direction gravitated to the teachings of the Five-Percent Nation. Rappers like the Wu-Tang Clan, Rakim Allah, Big Daddy Kane, Brand Nubian, and a host of others, usually from New York City, came to adhere to the belief that the black man is the original man, the cream of planet earth—god.

And of the white man? The Five-Percent Nation believes that whites are devils crafted in a laboratory by an evil scientist named Yacub. Rakim Allah spells out the rest in his song "The Ghetto." He says, "Once upon a time they lived in caves, exiled from the original man and strayed away."[1] The group Brand Nubian actually had a white man with devil horns appear in one of their videos.

The "Lessons" taught that Christians worshiped a "mystery god" or a "spook," a deity who can neither be seen nor heard in the physical realm and therefore can't be real.

WHITE MAN'S RELIGION

Many blacks who had grown up in a society where white imperialism, domination, and racism had greatly impaired their opportunities rejected Christianity for many of the same reasons that my young peers embraced the Five-Percent Nation. The image of Jesus as a white man with flowing blond locks, which to this day still adorns many black churches, proved unacceptable to them. You may say to yourself, *Oh, it's just a picture*. But you're wrong. It is so much more.

Consider the words that young Muhammad Ali offered while addressing college students in 1967. "See, we have been brainwashed. Everything good and of authority was made white. We look at Jesus, we see a white with blond hair and blue eyes. We look at all the angels, we see white with blond hair and blue eyes. Now, I'm sure if there's a heaven in the sky and the colored folks die and go to heaven, where are the colored angels? They must be in the kitchen preparing the milk and honey."[2]

The Boondocks is an adult cartoon, a satire that deals with themes most polite people won't discuss in mixed company. Real-life politicians, preachers, and media personalities appear in this comedy; their identities are thinly veiled by the change of a letter in a name. One of the most interesting characters is a regular named Uncle Ruckus. Ruckus is an African American who denies his ethnic heritage. He refers to other blacks as "n—s" and "d—s." Ruckus starts each day with prayer, but not necessarily to the Almighty that you know. Ruckus says, "I start by thanking the white man for the sunrise, for the land I walk on, for the air I breathe."[3]

In one episode, Uncle Ruckus dies and ends up in the afterlife. At the gates of paradise sits his hero, Ronald Reagan, in a white ten-gallon cowboy hat, driving a white chariot led by a team of white horses. Astonished, Ruckus asks the late president if he is in heaven.

"Not just heaven, Ruckus, white heaven," the former president answers. "You see there are many different types of people, Ruckus, so God created many separate but, well, for the most part, equal heavens."

Reagan goes on to explain, "White heaven is for decent, good, God-fearing Christians who just happen to, well, hate everything related to black people. That means no Muhammad Ali, no hip-hop music and no f—ing Jesse Jackson. . . . Turns out that God doesn't have much of a problem with racism. He doesn't even remember slavery, except in February."

As Reagan and Uncle Ruckus ride through the clouds, the discussion continues. Reagan admits his hatred of black people and then asks Uncle Ruckus if he knows why God has rewarded him so richly. Reagan says, "Because God loves white people, and if you teach everyone on earth to love the white man, you too can join us in white heaven."

To accentuate his point, Reagan touches Uncle Ruckus's forehead with his index finger. A greater miracle than Uncle Ruckus could have ever conjured in his tortured imagination comes to reality. For just a moment in time, Uncle Ruckus is transformed into a white man.

"Praise 'White God!'" he exclaims.

Now he's off on his mission. Uncle Ruckus is an evangelist on a mission to teach blacks and whites to hate black skin, to renounce blackness, and to embrace the "white God" and "his son, white Jesus."

When interviewed by a newscaster about his peculiar take on the Christian faith, Ruckus begins by saying, "First of all, white man, let me say that I love you, honor you, envy you, enjoy your smell, and I celebrate you in the name of white Jesus."

There is some truth in Uncle Ruckus's take on religion. The Christian faith and its lived reality in America have been a stew of truth, redemption, hypocrisy, innocent bloodshed, and radical racial brainwashing. Often the lines between faith and false witness blur in the shadows of a white deity. This brand of

Christianity can influence people of color to worship white people and at the same time bathe in self-hatred.

Years ago, I knew an older African American gentleman who had much in common with the fictional Uncle Ruckus. He once shared with me his rationale for the slave trade in which a continent was decimated and millions died. "The white man brought you Jesus," he said.

Jomo Kenyatta, the first president of Kenya, had a different take on it. Kenyatta saw religion through the eyes of one whose people had to fight to overthrow the oppression of colonialism. Kenyatta said, "When the missionaries arrived, the Africans had the land and the missionaries had the Bible. They taught us how to pray with our eyes closed. When we opened them, they had the land and we had the Bible."[4]

INTRODUCING JESUS

It is early morning on the shores of Ghana, West Africa, in the eighteenth century. Slaves are herded from their dark pens. Almost in unison, they squint at the sunlight as it filters through the clouds. Like cattle, they have been sequestered in crowded concrete pens for close to a month. Meals have consisted of a stinking, nameless slop poured into a feeding trough. Younger women have been separated from the pack and turned into unwilling concubines for the sailors, a rough and rowdy bunch from the back streets of a European slum.

The blacks are tied and marched like a slow, sad parade to the banks of the Atlantic Ocean. The sailors grunt commands in a foreign language. Blacks who hesitate are jabbed with bayonet points.

At the edge of the water, a huge wooden ship waits. The captain signals for the blacks to be brought aboard. Fear becomes universal. The sailors prod, push, and stab. As the first black climbs aboard, a priest proclaims, "Your name is Peter." The second is awarded a name he doesn't understand: John. With each name, a sprinkle of holy water is flung in the direction of the slave. And for the first time the Africans hear the name of the new, powerful God in whose name they have been kidnapped, raped, branded, and beaten. That deity's name is Jesus Christ.

In fact, Queen Elizabeth I once made a gift of the good ship *Jesus*. This *Jesus* was not the ark of salvation; it was crafted and designed to transport brown-skinned people from the shores of Africa to hell on earth, a place called America. The sea captain awarded the ship was so ruthless and notorious that his name eventually became synonymous with slavery itself: Captain John Hawkins.

Evangelist, can you imagine trying to explain the love and mercy of Jesus Christ to captives who have nearly lost their minds chained in the dank, filthy bowels of the ship called *Jesus*?

John Henrik Clarke is one of the most highly revered African American thinkers. The celebrated Pan-African historian, author, college professor, social critic, and activist was a Sunday school teacher when he began researching his African heritage. It was more the pictures of white Jesus than the theology itself that prompted his quest. He believed the pictures were instruments of oppression aimed at mind control. He believed that the images of Middle Eastern people transformed to whites helped blacks to accept their own subjugation at the hands of whites.

Dr. Clarke once asked, "How can the slave and the master worship the same God? Then both of them expect their prayers to be answered by the very same God?"[5] In a speech titled "Christianity Before Christ—African Spirituality," he says, "The European made Christianity a rationale for his prejudice and enslavement of the people."[6] In another speech he said,

Nearly all religions were brought to people and imposed on people by conquerors and used as the framework to control their minds. My main point here is that if you are a child of God and God is a part of you, then in your imagination God is supposed to look like you. And when you accept the picture of the deity assigned to you by another people, you become the spiritual prisoners of that people.[7]

Howard University professor Cain Hope Felder seems to draw the same conclusions in his book *Troubling Biblical Waters*. However, he believes that the images damaged not only African Americans but also black people all over the African diaspora.

The Jesus of the Bible bore no resemblance to the blond, blue-eyed portraits in Sunday school books and on the walls of church basements and homes. However, as foreign lands were conquered in the name of the Europeans' god, the image of that God came across the seas with the clergy. The conquerors used the blond, blue-eyed Jesus portrait to "prove" that they had been created in the very image of the God they worshiped.

CURSED BY GOD

Joshua 9:23 says, "You are now under a curse: You will never be released from service as woodcutters and water carriers for the house of my God." This curse was originally applied to Canaan, but American slaveholders attached it to Ham, the father of black humanity according to the post-flood Table of Nations in Genesis. For some, because Ham was damned to slavery, it followed that all black people would be under the same curse. I once had an African American talk radio host ask me in a live broadcast if black people were indeed cursed and damned to be in bondage as the "Scriptures say." He was earnest. I was mortified.

That afternoon, I outlined for him the presence of black people in the Bible. He was astounded. He had never heard those biblical facts before. It took that knowledge base to alleviate the darkness from his eyes and subsequently to open his heart to the possibility of a Jesus who loved him and desired a relationship with him.

Historian William Moseley wrote in his book *What Color Was Jesus?*:

> The image of Jesus Christ as White festers at the heart of White racism, the belief and/or practice of racial superiority. It can take many forms: individual or institutional, systemic or systematic, overt or covert, conscious or unconscious. It plays itself out in the forms of prejudice, discrimination, segregation, oppression, exploitation, and genocide.[8]

Missionaries of every Christian denomination set about to proselytize Native Americans and blacks with mixed results. Some mission societies stood staunchly against the idea of baptizing blacks, reasoning that if Paul's edict that the faith took down barriers been Jew and Greek, slaves and free, and male and female was true (Galatians 3:28), baptism into the Christian faith might dictate that equality would then exist between blacks and whites. Adherence to that belief would basically be the end of slavery.

THE RISE OF WHITE JESUS

The image of Jesus as a white man gained widespread prominence after the Civil War. In their book *The Color of Christ: The Son of God and the Saga of Race in America*, Edward J. Blum and Paul Harvey list reasons for this occurrence.[9] First, prior to the Civil War whiteness was associated with freedom and black skin with slavery. The Emancipation Proclamation changed that. White supremacists looking to reassert their authority thought it wise to now equate the whiteness of Jesus with their cause: hence, the Christian Knights of the Ku Klux Klan. That was pretty effective. If you were black, even if you couldn't read, you knew what a burning cross on your lawn represented and who had put it there.

D. W. Griffith's 1915 film *The Birth of a Nation* was as popular as *Star Wars* in its day. It was so innovative that movie makers still borrow elements of its cinematography. The film ends with Union and Confederate soldiers fighting together to defend their "Aryan birthright." The last scene shows a white Jesus superimposed over the screen, celebrating the rise of both the white Knights of the Ku Klux Klan and their god, a white Jesus.

Industrialization also figured into the rise of the Anglo image of Jesus. Pictures of Jesus could now be mass produced, imported, and exported throughout the world. Catholic immigrants from Eastern Europe brought pictures of the white Jesus with them to the New World.

In 1941, Warner Sallman's painting *Head of Christ* changed the world. Perhaps you have a copy of it on your wall. It certainly adorned the wall of my home as a child. The image of Jesus Christ with long, flowing brown hair, a beard, and blue eyes is the most famous piece of American art ever made. By 1944, more than fourteen million reproductions were sold. Today half a billion reproductions of this image are in print.

THE BIBLE GOES TO THE MOVIES

Some of the biggest box office hits of all time were derived from Bible stories. In 1956, Cecil B. DeMille's film *The Ten Commandments* was billed as the "Greatest Event in Motion Picture History." Charlton Heston played Moses, Yul Brynner played Rameses, and Anne Baxter played Nefretiri. What do they have in common? None of them have roots in the Middle East or Africa. In fact, they are all of European descent.

In 1963, actress Elizabeth Taylor was paid a record-breaking one million dollars to play the role of Cleopatra in the movie *Cleopatra*. Taylor in no way resembled an Egyptian. Her ancestry was European.

When Ridley Scott made the decision to name Welsh actor Christian Bale to play the part of the Hebrew Moses in his 2014 epic *Exodus: Gods and Kings*, there was some backlash. Scott responded that every Egyptian he'd ever known was white. And Ridley, with the benefit of the thousands of years of scholarship at his fingertips, decided to portray blacks as thieves, assassins, and, of course, slaves. Ridley's choice for God's representative in the film is certainly an odd one: the angel who emerges from the burning bush is a young white child with a British cockney accent.

And then, of course, there is Jesus himself. In 1961, Jeffrey Hunter, a white fellow from Louisiana, played Jesus in the movie

King of Kings. In 1966, Max Von Sydow played Jesus in *The Greatest Story Ever Told*. In 1999, Bale played Jesus in the TV movie *Mary, Mother of Jesus*. 2004's *The Passion of the Christ* is one of the most widely viewed films about Jesus, and many of the background players in Mel Gibson's classic are of Middle Eastern heritage. Yet Jim Caviezel, the man chosen to play the Son of God, is white. Coincidence?

THE TRUTH ABOUT ANCIENT AFRICA

The great chronicler of the ancient world, Herodotus (484–425 BC) traveled to Africa on a fact-finding expedition. Before the inter-marriage with foreign nations and intermingling with captured people, he said that the people he met in Egypt were "black and wooly-haired." He described the hair on the heads of the people in the lands below Egypt, which would be present-day Sudan, as "very wooly."[10]

Count Constantine de Volney, author of *Ruins of Empires*, after having visited the region where the great sphinx lay looking at the sunset, said, "I think that a race of black men who today are slaves and the object of our contempt is the same one to whom we owe our arts, sciences and even the very use of speech."[11]

Famed historian Yosef Ben-Jochannan later taught that Napoleon Bonaparte's troops blew off the Sphinx's nose with cannon fire during the French invasion of Egypt because they abhorred its African features.[12]

BLACK PEOPLE IN THE BIBLE

I attended a Christian fundamentalist junior high school. In the seventh grade, one of the most intelligent young people in the entire school looked at me and said, "It's the strangest thing about *you* people. Blacks have never contributed anything of significance to the history of the world." I just stared at him blankly. I was reading the same books he studied. And surely there were no illustrations of any people of color in those books, nor any mention of our contributions to history. So, I just walked away carrying my internalized shame. I carried it with me until I was a grown man in possession of a library card.

In the library, I discovered that in the ancient world the land below Egypt was called Ethiopia, Cush, Kush, Nubia, and Kemet. Ethiopia was translated "Land of the Blacks." The book *Africa's Glorious Legacy* tells us:

> Early Egyptians knew Nubia by various names, including Ta-Seti (Land of the Bow), Yam, and Wawat. Later Egyptian chronicles and the Bible called it Kush. Ancient historians knew Kush as the nation that conquered Egypt in the eighth century BC and ruled it for 60 years. Greeks and Romans labeled it Aethiopia, or "Land of the Burnt Faces."[13]

Although Cush is called Ethiopia in the Bible, it was not the Ethiopia that we speak of today. It was the land that we now refer to as Sudan.

In 2 Kings 18, Israel is under siege. Sennacherib, king of the Assyrians, headed a war machine unrivaled in the known world. His army came complete with battering rams, wall-scaling parties, cavalry, soldiers, and archers who could turn the sky black with arrows.

Judah too was vastly outnumbered. King Hezekiah had little more than a prayer to hold off the Assyrian army. That is why

Sennacherib poses this question to Hezekiah, "You say you have the counsel and the might for war—but you speak only empty words. On whom are you depending, that you rebel against me?" (2 Kings 18:20).

To protect itself militarily, ancient Egypt exerted military dominance over its neighbors. The people of Nubia and the nation of Cush were forced to pay tribute to the pharaohs. Nubian archers went north as conscripted soldiers in time of war.

In 725 BC, Piye, king of Nubia, started his conquest north toward Egypt, and he defeated four Egyptian kings. This was the dawn of Egypt's Twenty-Fifth Dynasty. Second Kings 19:9 says, "Now Sennacherib received a report that Tirhakah, the king of Cush, was marching out to fight against him."

Earlier, Sennacherib tried to discourage Hezekiah from depending on Tirhakah's help, referring to him as "Pharaoh king of Egypt" (2 Kings 18:21).

Without an understanding of the times, you might think that the chronicler of this epic is speaking of two separate monarchs. He is not. Having overrun Egypt, Tirhakah of Cush is both king of Cush and pharaoh of Egypt. He wore a crown with the symbol of two snakes, one for Cush and the other from Egypt. Meanwhile, the bloodthirsty Assyrian monarch Sennacherib embarked on a scorched-earth campaign.

Sennacherib attacked the fortified cities of Judah and captured them. In those dark days, King Hezekiah sent a message to Sennacherib acquiescing to blackmail. Sennacherib made the price high. In order to pay it, Hezekiah had to give all of the silver in the temple as ransom money. If that wasn't enough, he had to empty the royal treasury of silver. It still wasn't enough. As a final measure, Hezekiah had the gold stripped from the doors and door-posts of God's holy temple and sent to Sennacherib. Can you imagine what the enemies of Israel whispered when they heard the news? Sennacherib was not finished. He sent word that he was going to capture the entire nation of Israel. With all hope lost, King Hezekiah did two things. First, he called upon the Lord God. Second, he called on the only military force on earth capable of facing down the Assyrian threat.

Second Kings 19:9 says, "Now Sennacherib received a report that Tirhakah, the king of Cush, was marching out to fight against him." Earlier in the chapter, he tries to discourage Hezekiah from depending on his help referring to him in verse 21 as "Pharaoh of Egypt."

Piankhi conquered much of Egypt. His nephew Tirhakah controlled both Nubia and Egypt by this time. He had defeated the Assyrians in previous battles.

Herodotus, famed historian of the ancient world, wrote that Pharaoh Tirhakah's gods came to him in a dream and told him to "march boldly out" against the Assyrians to protect Israel. Henry T. Aubin, author of *The Rescue of Jerusalem*, believes that the Assyrian king's withdrawal from Jerusalem came upon hearing the rumor that Pharaoh Tirhakah and the Cushite forces were marching toward Israel. Aubin continues, "For our purposes what is important is that this historian of the fifth century BC depicts the Kushite-Egyptian forces, on the very eve of the showdown, as anticipating an all-out battle. It is also important that Herodotus states that the next day the Kushite-Egyptian army was in hot pursuit of the retreating enemy."[14]

In Judah's darkest hour, it turned to Tirhakah. You'll probably never see anyone who looks like Tirhakah, the king of Egypt and

Ethiopia, portrayed in an epic about Egypt. However, statues and paintings show that his skin was a deep brown, his nose broad, his lips thick. If you painted a picture of Tirhakah with modern clothes on, no one would mistake him for anything other than a black man.

WAS JESUS BLACK?

Was Jesus a black man? During American slavery, slave masters often created children with slave women. The children born of these unions would be born into slavery. The famed abolitionist Frederick Douglass and Booker T. Washington, founder of Tuskegee University, both had white fathers who were slaveholders. However, they were both considered black by society. Walter Plecker, a registrar of Virginia's Bureau of Vital Statistics, codified what became known as the "one drop rule" in 1924. It stated that one drop of black blood made a person black. That train of thought still lives today. When Barack Obama was elected president, it was said that he was the first black president, even though his mother was 100 percent white.

In his book *The Black Presence in the Bible*, Walter Arthur McCray does a thorough breakdown of the Table of Nations recorded in Genesis 10. According to that Scripture passage, Noah's son Ham became the progenitor of black humanity. McCray tells us that the name Ham means "'hot,' 'heat' and by application, 'black.'" In antiquity, Africa was known as the "land of Ham."[15]

In Genesis 10:6, we find that Ham, the father of black humanity, was blessed with four sons: Cush, Put, Egypt, and Canaan. Matthew 1:3 tells us that Tamar, a descendant of Ham's son Canaan, was one of Jesus' forbears. Rahab, the commercially sexually exploited woman who hid the two Israelite spies, was also a daughter of Canaan and a descendant of Ham. Finally, Bathsheba, the mother of Solomon, was first married to Uriah the Hittite. According to McCoy, the Hittites were also descendants of Ham. If Jesus Christ lived in human form today in America, the "one drop" rule would designate him a black man.

CONFUSION AND SHAME

Years ago I invited a friend to visit my church home. I'm sure he had visited many churches with stained glass images of a European Jesus sporting long, flowing brown locks. My home church's image of Christ showed a man with flowing robes and a beard, in some ways very similar to the one that hangs in churches all over the world. The only difference is that the Jesus in our church is clearly of African descent.

My friend was outraged. He thought the image was the height of blasphemy. It was all he could do to sit there until the benediction was proclaimed. Later, we discussed the issue. As he sputtered his fury, he would not even refer to the image as Jesus. In his lengthy diatribe he could only say, "That picture . . . that picture." What made his rage even more difficult to understand was the fact that his own flesh was much darker than the stained glass image of Jesus. Yet he despised that image. Could it have been he hated it so because he despised his own blackness?

One of the most curiously titled books I own is *Don't Call Me Black Because I'm a Spirit* by Marty Grace. In the second sentence Grace informs us that the book was written under the direction of God's Holy Spirit: "All [the devil] wants to do is cause confusion in the church. We cannot allow that to continue. Stop running around like some of the preachers I know boasting about their color! You are not a person of color any more to God. Some people are the only ones concerned about their color—not God."[16]

The premise of his book is that once people accept Christ as their Savior, they are free of the burden of race. From that moment on, they are spirit and not flesh. The blood of Christ washes our sins and our skin. As Pastor Grace informs us, "We are a new species, a distinct kind of people. Therefore, stop following the world. And let's lead the world back to God, their creator."

At one point Grace says, "I know some people might say I'm a little off my rocker because I go around saying that I'm not black."[17]

I don't doubt his mental faculties. As deeply as I disagree with him, I believe that Grace is as sane as you or me. You see, I've talked with many people who share his desire to simply be known as "spirit." Many believe that the blood of Jesus Christ washed away not only the blackness of sin but the blackness of skin. And they were happy to be free of both!

MALCOLM X

Whereas Marty Grace holds a belief that Christian people of color should ignore their ethnic heritage, Malcolm X held an entirely different point of view. As Christian preachers downplayed the issue of racism and the hypocrisy of the church in the face of lynching, Malcolm X held up a mirror to faith institutions. At the same time, he told black people to explore their heritage and to be proud of it.

Malcolm X is one of the few figures in history recognizable by either his first or last name alone. If you were to walk into a soul food restaurant in your local city and say the name Malcolm, most everyone would know who you're referring to. If you were to walk in sporting a baseball cap with an X on the front, most people would think of the same individual. Ironically, he had been given another name by the time he died. After having made his pilgrimage to Mecca, his name became El Hajj Malik El Shabazz. He died with that name.

Malcolm's life and journey are celebrated throughout the African diaspora. The epic motion picture *Malcolm X* closes with South African president Nelson Mandela quoting one of Malcolm's most famous speeches: "We declare our right on this earth to be a man, to be a human being, to be respected as a human being, to be given the rights of a human being in this society, on this earth, in this day, which we intend to bring into existence *by any means necessary*."[18] The phrase "by any means necessary" was considered so threatening that filmmaker Spike Lee cuts off Mandela's voice and splices Malcolm's image and voice into the film's last seconds to say those words.

Malcolm X was born Malcolm Little in Lansing, Michigan, on May 19, 1925. His father and mother were strong adherents to the black nationalist teachings of Marcus Garvey, who led the most populous black organization that has ever existed. The UNIA (United Negro Improvement Association) slogan was "Up, you mighty race. You can accomplish what you will." Garvey's teachings must have seemed radical for the times. In the days when lynchings were an everyday occurrence in America, he preached black empowerment and black reliance. Garvey preached black pride and called for black people all over the world to embrace all things African and to stand together.

Malcolm's father was an evangelist for the cause. He became despised in a social order that would have seemed a threat if its poor, disinherited, and oppressed citizens came together and declared their common humanity. So, one night Earl Little went out and never returned home. When they found him, his body had been almost severed in half by the iron wheels of a street car.

This disaster left his widow completely unprepared to meet the task of being the breadwinner of the home. She suffered a mental collapse and wound up in a mental institution. Meanwhile, her children were farmed out to the foster-care system. Malcolm's troubled youth and young adulthood is thoroughly documented in the *Autobiography of Malcolm X*, one of the most read books in the black history pantheon.

THE NATION

In January 1946, twenty-one-year-old Malcolm (then known in the streets by the moniker Detroit Red) caught three concurrent eight-to-ten-year sentences, effectively ending his run as a hustler, pimp, drug dealer, number runner, and burglary artist. He wasn't happy. Manning Marable wrote, "During his first months, Malcolm routinely insulted guards and prisoners alike. He had never been particularly religious, but now he concentrated his profanities against God and religion in general. Other prisoners, listening to Malcolm's tirades, came up with a further nickname for him: 'Satan.'"[19]

While Malcolm was raising hell in the penitentiary, a number of his siblings on the outside had come under the sway of the teachings of the Nation of Islam. According to these teachings, God had come to Detroit at the height of the Great Depression in the form of Master Fard Muhammad, a seller of silk scarves.

Opposite to everything that they had been taught since the cradle, Master Fard told the economically desolate refugees from the American South that God himself was a black man. The theology went on to note that the white man was actually an irredeemable devil genetically disposed to violence and oppression. He was grafted from a germ in a scientific experiment gone horribly wrong on the island of Patmos by an evil scientist with an unusually large head named Yacub. One day, Fard Muhammad vanished from the streets of Detroit never again to be seen by his followers. His most ardent disciple, the Honorable Elijah Muhammad, rose up to lead the flock. At the urging of his family members, Malcolm began to correspond with Elijah Muhammad. Before Malcolm left prison in 1952, he replaced his surname with X. The X separated him from the name given to his family by its slave owners generations earlier.

Malcolm X entered the iron house a hustler and a coke addict. When he was released, he was an austere Muslim minister. He ate but one meal a day. He wore suits daily. He didn't smoke or do drugs. He didn't use profanity. His life was given completely to absorbing and disseminating the teachings of the Nation of Islam. It didn't take long for those around him to discover that Malcolm was a charismatic and gifted speaker. He quickly rose in the ranks of ministry, eventually being named the minister of Muhammad's Temple Number 7 in Harlem, New York, perhaps the most high-profile house of worship in the Nation of Islam.

FISHING FOR SOULS

Few have ever considered the tremendous impact that Malcolm X had on the way people all over the world view the practice of

Christianity. Malcolm held the church up to an iridescent light like a flawed diamond and meticulously pointed out its sins toward black humanity. While the Christian preacher told his flock that the images of white Jesus were of no consequence and should not even be considered, Malcolm had another message: "Only the poor, brainwashed American Negro has been made to believe that Christ was white, to maneuver him into worshiping the white man."[20]

On Sundays, he and his followers would stand outside of churches seeking to persuade members to move away from their churches.

> The blond-haired, blue-eyed white man has taught you and me to worship a *white* Jesus, and to shout and sing and pray to this God that's *his* God, the white man's God. The white man has taught us to shout and sing and pray until we *die*, to wait until *death*, for some dream heaven-in-the-hereafter, when we're *dead*, while the white man has his milk and honey in the streets paved with golden dollars right here on *this* earth!

He went on to say,

> Christianity is the white man's religion. The Holy Bible in the white man's hands and his interpretations of it have been the greatest single ideological weapon for enslaving millions of non-white human beings. Every country where the white man has conquered with guns, he has always paved the way, and salved the conscience, by carrying the Bible and interpreting it to call the people "heathens" and "pagans": then

he sends his guns, then his missionaries behind the guns to mop up.[21]

Malcolm had great respect for ministers like Harlem firebrand Adam Clayton Powell Jr. and Detroit's black nationalist pastor Albert Cleage Jr. of the Shrine of the Black Madonna. However, he generally saw hypocrisy in the fact that churches were segregated and that white ministers rarely used their pulpits and power to decry the lynching, poverty, and massive unemployment faced by black Christians. Combine that with the fact that many of the staunchest racists in America claimed allegiance to the Christian faith.

MALCOLM AND BLACK HISTORY

Malcolm was a voracious student of black history. Early on, he understood that the slaveholders told their black servants that they had no history, that Africa was a place where they were picked from trees by benevolent white people who wanted to give them a better life in the cotton fields of the United States. Malcolm said, "This was that crime that was committed—he convinced us that our people back home were savages and animals in the jungle, and the reason we couldn't talk was because we never had a language. And we grew up thinking that we never had one."[22]

Malcolm taught his followers that historians' studies were biased. He said, "This tricky white man was able to take the Egyptian civilization, write books about it, put pictures in those books, make movies for television and the theater—so skillfully that he has even convinced other white people that the ancient Egyptians were white people themselves."[23]

Malcolm believed that the most grievous sin committed against black people was the stripping of their names. The fact that the slavers provided names for their chattel was an abomination and a perpetuation of the legacy of slavery to Malcolm.

According to Malcolm X, black self-hatred began with the slave enterprise. In order to make it work, the slave owners had to make blacks fight each other. Light-skin slaves were pitted against dark-skin slaves, and both were taught to loathe the African continent. Malcolm mused,

Now what effect does [the struggle over Africa] have on us? Why should the Black man in America concern himself since he's been away from the African continent for three or four hundred years? Why should we concern ourselves? What impact does what happens to them have upon us? . . . You show me one of these people over here who has been thoroughly brainwashed and has a negative attitude toward Africa, and I'll show you one who has a negative attitude toward himself.[24]

Minister Malcolm X was very critical of many of the methods used by the leaders of the civil rights movement. He saved some of his most virulent criticisms for nonviolent revolutionaries like Dr. Martin Luther King Jr.:

Any Negro who teaches other Negroes to turn the other cheek is disarming that Negro. Any Negro who teaches Negroes to turn the other cheek in the face of attack is disarming that Negro of his God-given right, of his moral right, or his natural right, of his intelligent right to defend himself. Everything in nature can defend itself, and is right in defending itself, except the American Negro. And men like King—their job is to go among Negroes and teach Negroes "Don't fight back." He doesn't tell them, "Don't fight each other." "Don't fight the white man" is what he's saying in essence.[25]

Malcolm X was considered a bogeyman by most of his white contemporaries as well as some blacks who feared an outrageously outspoken black man. However, the black urban throngs adored him. He told black people they were beautiful. He told them they had a glorious past. Malcolm told his people they could rise if they stuck together, and they loved him for it.

On February 21, 1965, Malcolm X was gunned down in front of his family and well-wishers at the Audubon Ballroom in Upper Manhattan. At Malcolm's funeral, actor Ossie Davis ended his eulogy with these words:

Consigning these mortal remains to earth, the common mother of all, secure in the knowledge that what we place in the ground is no more now a man—but a seed—which, after the winter of discontent, will come forth again to meet us. And we will know him then for what he was and is—a Prince—our own black shining Prince!—who didn't hesitate to die, because he loved us so.[26]

Malcolm's influence infiltrated the civil rights movement, causing an ideological split between Martin Luther King Jr.'s old guard and the young lions led by Stokely Carmichael (later Kwame Ture) of the Student Nonviolent Coordinating Committee. As they marched from Selma to Montgomery, the young blacks began to chant "Black Power!" The Black Panther Party for Self-Defense rose from the streets of Oakland on the shoulders of Malcolm's powerful thoughts and rhetoric. Malcolm influenced a generation of black Christian ministers, perhaps foremost among them theologian James Cone, who wrote the seminal work *Black Theology and Black Power*. Malcolm's autobiography has sold millions of copies. Each time it is read, part of Malcolm X lives again.

WHERE DO WE GO FROM HERE?

We have to shake off the apathy that stops us from doing our due diligence concerning people of varying ethnic groups in the Bible. Scores of people have walked away from the Christian faith because we've clung to the images of God's Son as a European white man. The resistance movement must confront the darkness of the past so the church can be viable for another generation of not only black people but progressive people of various ethnic groups. The resistance movement will take us to the library to study the histories of the people we minister to.

Thousands upon thousands of people have walked away from the Christian faith because of the image of Jesus portrayed as a white man. Thousands have walked away from a church that refused to decry racism. The resistance calls on us to raise our fists. It calls on us to call right, right and wrong, wrong. This is an upstream swim, but it must be made.

This chapter brought up some questions that only you can answer. What should we do with the images of white Jesus that are still in church windows and church walls all over the country?

HOMEWORK

- Write an essay based on the following questions: How has white supremacy woven itself into the gospel presented to people of color over the centuries? Why does this knowledge of the past sometimes become a barrier to evangelism in some quarters?

- For extra credit gather friends together to watch the 1992 film *Malcolm X*, starring Denzel Washington, or another Denzel film titled *Cry Freedom*. Discuss the insights you gather.

TRUE RELIGION

*The Black Church and
the Resistance*

E arly on, slaveholders understood the primacy and persuasiveness of religion in the slave quarters. They feared black religion and sought to control and suppress it. Faith and hope are dangerous companions in the heart of someone who is supposed to live like a brute animal. For the slave, religion was often a great tool of resistance.

In his book *A Fire in the Bones*, Albert J. Raboteau writes,

> British colonists in North America proved especially indifferent if not downright hostile, to the conversion of their slaves. At first, opposition was based on the suspicion that English law forbade the enslavement of Christians and so would require slaveholders to emancipate any slave who received baptism. Masters suspected that slaves would therefore seek to be baptized in order to gain freedom. These fears were quickly allayed by colonial legislation declaring baptism did not alter the state of the enslaved.[1]

African people might not have been Christians upon landing on the shores of the Americas in chains. However, they were religious people. As they began to adopt the Christian faith, they brought elements of African culture to the pulpit. They took the master's hymns and added rhythm. Shouting, stomping, and handclapping were added to formerly staid 4/4 hymns. When their masters saw how deeply the blacks were drawn to religion, they imported white ministers to their plantations to deliver the Sunday morning sermon.

The slaves were nothing if not inventive. Beyond the master's watchful gaze, they would steal away to the swamps and back-woods to host their own unsanctioned church services. How they escaped detection is a mystery because this service was *loud*. The spirituals were born here. Women would break out in ecstatic praise. Sometimes the slaves would gather in a circle and dance as a form of worship. At some point the leader would emerge. He was the pastor. It was illegal for the slaves to read, lest they gain knowledge of their plight or read enough of the Bible to find that God fought on behalf of slaves. Somehow, however, the preacher would know enough of the Bible to grasp those points. His favorite sermon might come from the book of Exodus. He reasoned that if God wanted the children of Israel freed, why not the blacks in America?

Knowledge of the Bible made the slaves rebellious, restless, and dissatisfied, which is why it was illegal for slaves to learn how to read, particularly the preacher. If master wanted to find out who had ordered his fields burned down, he need not look farther than the preacher's cabin. If he wanted to find out who was behind a bloody insurrection, he found the same address. The pastor was the slaves' most adored and respected slave on the plantation. He was also often the most despised and feared figure by whites.

The preacher was more than likely the most courageous slave on the plantation. If gunfire was coming, it was going to strike the preacher first.

Richard Allen was born on a Delaware plantation on February 14, 1760. Early on, he felt the call to preach the Word of God. When Allen's owner, Stokely Sturgis, became convinced that slavery was wrong, he offered his slaves a chance to buy their freedom. Allen did extra work to earn the money and bought his freedom in 1780. He moved to Philadelphia, where he became a respected leader in the African American community.

St. George's Church, which Allen attended, was segregated. One Sunday, Allen and a number of his fellow believers of brown hue knelt in the "whites only" section. All hell broke loose. Church leaders physically removed them from their knees. Allen recalled opening his eyes during the prayer time to find fellow African American minister Reverend Absalom Jones being physically seized by church leaders. Later he recalled, "I raised my head up and saw one of the trustees, H— M—, having hold of the Rev. Absalom Jones, pulling him up off of his knees and saying, 'You must get up—you must not kneel here.' Mr. Jones replied, 'wait until prayer is over.' Mr. H— M— said 'no, you must get up now, or I will call for aid and force you away.'"[2] Richard Allen and the members of the black community who followed took the message to heart. They left St. George's Church en masse that day. This incident led them to found the African Methodist Episcopal Church.

Segregation is a social arrangement that has plagued the black church since the first blacks landed on American shores. Slave masters would take their chattel to churches with balconies nicknamed "N—r Heaven." African Americans were completely barred from some churches. This problem launched the African American church. However, the black church was much more than an alternative. It was a living, breathing, evolving organism, the most powerful institution created by black people in America.

THE BLACK CHURCH

The black church was birthed in the belly of struggle. Its first act of resistance was to defy one of the great ideals that kept slavery in place. Slaves were often separated by language, either in the holds of the ships that brought them here or on the plantations they were sold to. It did not benefit the master to see the slaves develop kinship. At any moment he wanted to be free to sell family members. Therefore, he did not allow them to have legal marriages. The slaves rebelled by creating church families. They rebelled against the master's wishes to destroy their self-esteem by giving each other church titles like "head deacon" or "mother of the usher board."

In the Antebellum South, the black preacher talked about a freedom that could be had before one touched the golden streets of heaven. The preachers not only talked about it, they were willing to die for it. The Underground Railroad that carried black Southerners to freedom was in part an extension of the black church.

On August 21, 1831, Nat Turner, an African American slave minister, led a slave uprising. He and his army, which included some free blacks, cut a bloody swath across Southampton County, Virginia. Before the uprising was quelled, sixty whites and one-hundred-twenty blacks were dead. In the wake of the slaughter, the black church was banned and outlawed in certain regions of the South. Still, the teachings pushed blacks to resist and rebel.

Speaking to a black convention audience in 1843, Rev. Henry Highland Garnet made a memorable call for the forceful overthrow of slavery. He said, "Now is the day and the hour. Let every slave throughout the land do this, and the days of slavery are numbered. You cannot be more oppressed than you have been—you cannot suffer greater cruelties than you have already. Rather die free men than live to be slaves. . . . Let your motto be resistance! Resistance! Resistance!"[3]

From its very inception, long before the birth of Martin Luther King Jr., the black church preached not only hope for the afterlife but also human rights and better life for people of color right here.

THE SACRED BALANCE

From the beginning the black church has balanced between the two spheres of black theology, the dialectic of the priestly and the prophetic traditions. The priestly side of the faith deals with Communion, baptism, marriage, and salvation. The prophetic deals with God's connection to the affairs of human beings, including justice issues. That's why no one thought it strange when a minister taught his members that they would have to fight for freedom and later fight for the vote and equal rights.

For the blacks, no area of human life was untouched from the hand and will of God. After the abolition of slavery, African American churches sprang up all over the United States. Poor black Christians put pennies together and created colleges, funded banks, and built mutual-aid societies.

The church was where black people could be themselves. It restored the bonds of family that had been broken by the slave trade. Everyone was either "brother" or "sister," and all were one. They were fond of quoting the Scripture, "In Christ there is neither Jew nor Gentile, neither slave nor free" (Galatians 3:28). George Lighty might have been called "boy" at the café where he washed floors, but he was Deacon Lighty in church. Black people called the shots, made the rules, paid the preacher, and owned the building. The black church was the center of not only spiritual but social life. It was revered.

Peter J. Paris writes in *The Social Teaching of the Black Churches*:

> Clearly, the black Christian tradition has been the lifeline of the black community. It alone has constituted the ground for their claims of humanity and, as such, has always placed blacks in opposition to the prevailing ethos of the larger American society. Apart from the tradition it is doubtful that blacks would have been able to survive the dehumanizing force of chattel slavery and its legacy of racism.[4]

THE CIVIL RIGHTS MOVEMENT

A book of this sort does not have the bandwidth to cover the important history of the civil rights movement, history so essential that any minister of the gospel should become acquainted with it. However, I will touch on it briefly.

Ralph Abernathy's autobiography, *And the Walls Came Tumbling Down*, takes the readers inside the civil rights movement. He recalls the night of the first mass meeting following the arrest of Rosa Parks in Montgomery, Alabama:

As we drove through the darkened streets we told each other the people would turn out, but we really didn't believe it. About five blocks away from the church we saw cars parked on both sides of the street; and when we were about three blocks away, the driveways and front yards were also filled up. First we thought it was a party, then Martin and I came to the conclusion simultaneously—somebody extremely important had died, the head deacon or the preacher himself.[5]

As they drew closer to the church, they heard the roar of many voices. The great civil rights leader said, "When we round the last corner we saw them, milling in the dark shadows of the overhanging oaks—hordes of people, an army of them, more people than I had ever seen in my life."[6]

This was not the beginning of the civil rights movement. That campaign had actually started before Abernathy was born. However, that night saw the birth of a movement led for the most part by clergy, centered in church buildings, and based largely on Christian principles. Martin Luther King Jr. adapted some of Gandhi's principles that night to point the way toward the promised land. It would be a long, protracted journey, but the masses of black people would win their struggle for dignity in Montgomery, Alabama.

King believed in a God of justice who upheld the hands of the oppressed. He quoted from the Old Testament book of Amos. King took the story of the rich man and the beggar and crafted it in his hands like a porcelain maker might form a piece of pottery. Followers with musical abilities took traditional hymns and turned them into freedom songs.

THE TWO JESUS CHRISTS

In the twentieth century, the church was a mainstay of the black community. Even people who were nominal members went to church on Christmas, Easter, and Mother's Day.

In the twenty-first century, American churches are experiencing an exodus. This is true of most mainstream African American churches as well. We must also take into account some of the lessons we learned in chapter six. Young blacks question a Christ whose image and name have been so interwoven with oppression and white supremacy.

Rev. Dr. J. Alfred Smith Sr. is an elder statesman of the black church, once named one of the greatest black preachers of our time by *Ebony* magazine. Smith said in an interview for this book:

> There are two Jesus Christs. There is the Jesus Christ of American patriotism and there is the Jesus Christ of liberation. I am a black liberation theologian. I follow the second of the two. I follow that gospel that deals with Jesus, a marginalized Jew, a Jew who had no voting rights, a Jew who could not become a citizen, a Jew who lived poor and died poor. Jesus' parents were Hebrew-speaking immigrants who went to Egypt, where they had to learn another language. This is the Christ that I speak of, not the American Christ whose theology justified land-stealing and genocide of Native American land.[7]

I do not serve the Christ who saw me as a commodity and went as far as to have the Constitution changed to declare me to be three-fifths of a human being. I fell in love with the Jesus of Luke 4:18-19, who says he came "to proclaim good news to the poor," "freedom for the prisoners" and "to set the oppressed free."

Now pastor emeritus of the Allen Temple Baptist Church of East Oakland, Dr. Smith is a warlord for social justice. He is a revolutionary pastor of a church of thousands who forged alliances with the Black Panther Party for Self-Defense and built a faith institution on the relevancy of black theology to the black community. For the duration of his ministry, he has had to defend the black church and black faith against virulent criticism. When asked about the fact that slave masters used Jesus Christ to chain the minds of their chattel, Smith responded,

> The slaves redeemed the religion that the slave masters had tainted. There is a certain absurdity to our faith. Western philosophers search for truth with the use of analytical process and an instance of empiricism. They use deconstruction to come up with the essence of reality. The black experience is more intuitive and more metaphysical. It relies on a seventh sense that enables us to survive the absurdity of our situation with our faith intact.

A PREACHER IS CHALLENGED

In the fall of 1935, Christian mystic Howard Thurman was sent on a friendship tour that took him to student groups in India, Burma, and Ceylon. After delivering an address at a law college, he was invited to have coffee with a senior college official. Away from the flash of cameras and listening ears, the Hindu educator asked bluntly,

> What are you doing over here? More than three hundred years ago your forefathers were taken from the western

coast of Africa as slaves. The people who dealt in the slave traffic were Christians. One of your famous Christian hymn writers, Sir John Newton, made his money from the sale of slaves to the New World. He is the man who wrote, "How Sweet the Name of Jesus Sounds" and "Amazing Grace"—there may be others, but these are the only ones I know. The name of one of the famous British slave vessels was "Jesus."

The men who brought the slaves were Christians. Christian ministers, quoting the Christian apostle Paul, gave sanction of religion to the system of slavery. . . . During all the period since then you have lived in a Christian nation in which you were segregated, lynched, and burned. Even in the church, I understand there is segregation. One of my students who went to your country sent me a clipping telling me about a Christian church in which the regular worship was interrupted so that many could join a mob against one of your fellows. When he had been caught and done to death, they came back to resume their worship of their Christian God.

The educator went on, "I do not wish to seem rude to you. But, sir, I think you are a traitor to all the darker peoples of the earth. I am wondering what you, an intelligent man, can say in defense of your position."[8]

Thurman's response became the groundbreaking book *Jesus and the Disinherited*. Some say that this treatise of fewer than one hundred pages launched the civil rights movement. It is said that Martin Luther King Jr. would not go anywhere without that book, even to jail.

Thurman wrote in *Jesus and the Disinherited*,

I can count on the fingers of one hand the number of times that I have heard a sermon on the meaning of religion, of Christianity, to the man who stands with his back against the wall. It is urgent that my meaning be crystal clear. The masses of men live with their backs constantly against the wall. They are the poor, the disinherited, the dispossessed. What does our religion say to them?[9]

If we can't answer this question, we will continue to lose ground. If you are looking down from the deck of an ocean liner at a nonswimmer who has fallen into the sea, that person doesn't want to hear your critique of Immanuel Kant's *Groundwork of the Metaphysics of Morals*. The nonswimmer is hollering for a life preserver or maybe for you to jump in and come to the rescue. Likewise, a message preached for people with their backs against the wall should include a detailed description of what the wall feels like and what it's made of. A message to someone who is poor, disinherited, and dispossessed starts with an understanding of forces pressing that person into the wall. That person has to know that you know he or she is oppressed. In order to break through, you can't ignore the fact that this person doesn't have this month's rent and begin to talk about heaven, where there will be no landlords. No, you must be able to outline the oppression and then speak to it. It is also important to convey this message to people in a way that squares with their worldview.

Jesus told people he had come that their joy might be full. He said he had come that his followers would have life more abundantly. He spoke forgiveness to the woman caught in adultery. He blessed the hungry with literal bread. He turned over tables when he saw injustice. What would this look like today in forgotten corners of America where people are hungry and neglected by society? What would this look like for gang members who are haunted by nightmares of things they got away with but still live with night and day? What would Jesus' message look like for parents dismayed by the third-class education their child is receiving from teachers who transition in and out of the classroom every three months? What would Jesus say to people who have asthma because their housing project was built on a toxic Superfund site? What would Jesus' words mean to a person who has been homeless for eight years?

These questions are not easily answered. However, there is a new generation of black clergy and lay members seeking solutions and rising to the challenges.

Some months ago I attended a meeting at Oakland City Hall where the issue of homelessness was being discussed, loudly. Black pastors were on their feet, not arguing but proposing solutions and offering to do the grunt work to make those solutions become reality. These faith leaders were offering to build what are known as "tiny houses" on their church properties so the ones Jesus referred to as the "least of these" could lay their heads down at night in peace and safety.

I have met black church members involved in every aspect of our struggle, from human trafficking to environmentalism. It doesn't take many people to make a change when God is involved. Often the pastors leading these struggles have fewer than fifty members in their congregations. Yet the tradition of the black church to fight for the black community continues unabated.

HOMEWORK

Howard Thurman said,

> I can count on the fingers of one hand the number of times
> that I have heard a sermon on the meaning of religion, of
> Christianity, to the man who stands with his back against the
> wall. It is urgent that my meaning be crystal clear. The masses
> of men live with their backs constantly against the wall.
> They are the poor, the disinherited, the dispossessed. What
> does our religion say to them?[10]

- Write a two-page essay about what the Christian faith says
  to the people he describes in the twenty-first century.

SOCIAL JUSTICE

Raise-Your-Fist Religion

G rowing up, I was no stranger to the church house. Trust me. I rarely missed Sunday school or church services. We often went back for the evening services. I attended Good News Club, Brigade Boys, and Wednesday night Bible study. In the summers I went to Bible camp. I also participated in the Bible Memory Association offerings. My upbringing taught me the way of holiness. It also centered on eternity.

When riots cut a fiery swath through a portion of the city when I was a boy, the pastor had no theology outside of sin and redemption to address the anger and frustration simmering in the ghetto across town. There were no sermons from the book of Amos. There was no talk of God's sense of justice or God's concern for the poor. The pastor spoke nothing about the income equality gap between blacks and whites or the soul-crushing poverty that people of color experienced ten city blocks from his church. When other pastors walked the riot-torn streets of the ghetto to speak with the residents in the wake of the rioting, our pastor stayed home. What was there to say?

I was a grown man in my twenties before I began to understand that God might have something to say about injustice in society.

I picked up a book about Martin Luther King Jr. titled *Bearing the Cross: Martin Luther King Jr. and the Southern Christian Leadership Conference*, by David J. Garrow. Then I read *Parting the Waters: America in the King Years, 1954–63*, by Taylor Branch. These books introduced me to the social aspects of Scripture. Through them, I began to understand that God is not just concerned about the afterlife. God is concerned about justice issues and how people live on the earth right now.

THE FORGOTTEN BIBLE

I began to read the Minor Prophets, who incidentally had been given minor attention in my church when I was a kid. The book of Amos, with its railing against economic inequality and oppression of the poor, opened my eyes. I read the book of Nehemiah. Nehemiah was a government official so concerned about the fallen condition of his home folks that he returned home to help rebuild the wall that protected his people and gave them dignity. Without an understanding of the fact that God is a God of justice who hates poverty and inequality, it will be difficult to serve in the 'hood.

The Wire is a fictionalized exploration of the institutions of the city of Baltimore: drug lords, gangs, the school system, and the press. The show explores the way that these inhuman and cruel institutions catch individuals between their gears. David Simon, the creator of the HBO series, says,

> [*The Wire*] was about people who were worth less and who were no longer necessary, as maybe 10 or 15% of my country is no longer necessary to the operation of the economy.

It was about them trying to solve, for lack of a better term, an existential crisis. In their irrelevance, their economic irrelevance, they were nonetheless still on the ground occupying this place called Baltimore and they were going to have to endure somehow.

That's the great horror show. What are we going to do with all these people that we've managed to marginalize?[1]

Luke 4:17-21 reports something that took place at the very beginning of Jesus' public ministry. He rose in the synagogue to read from the Torah. Scripture says,

> and the scroll of the prophet Isaiah was handed to him. Unrolling it, he found the place where it is written:
>
> The Spirit of the Lord is on me,
>> because he has anointed me
>> to proclaim good news to the poor.
> He has sent me to proclaim freedom for the prisoners
>> and recovery of sight for the blind,
> to set the oppressed free,
>> to proclaim the year of the Lord's favor.
>
> Then he rolled up the scroll, gave it back to the attendant and sat down. The eyes of everyone in the synagogue were fastened on him. He began by saying to them, "Today this scripture is fulfilled in your hearing."

Jesus proclaimed his messiahship by stating that God had anointed him to help the most marginalized people in society, that God had anointed him to massage salve into the wounds of those who were bruised. Today, the families of people slain by police might easily fall into that category in America.

Come, let us continue on our journey.

OPEN SEASON ON BLACK MALES

On February 26, 2012, seventeen-year-old Trayvon Martin was shot to death by a community safety officer named George Zimmerman. In the aftermath of his acquittal, three activists, Alicia Garza, Patrisse Cullors, and Opal Tometi, began to use the hashtag #BlackLivesMatter. Today, BLM is both a movement and an organization with a vision statement and a mission. Both the movement and the organization center on an outcry against police brutality and police abuse. In subsequent years, deadly video-taped confrontations between police and black men across the country have been vigorously protested by the Black Lives Matter movement.

On August 9, 2014, Officer Darren Wilson of the Ferguson, Missouri, Police Department stopped eighteen-year-old Michael Brown and a friend as they were walking down the street. Angry words were exchanged. A confrontation ensued. The unarmed teenager was shot to death. His body lay in the street for more than four hours before the coroner removed it. Witnesses said that young Michael had been executed by the officer. Protests ensued, which devolved into rioting. Police in paramilitary gear stormed the streets. Days of tear gas and marching followed. Mass arrests occurred.

In the coming days the Department of Justice would uncover a pattern of bias in the Ferguson Police Department's dealings with its African American citizens.

In 88 percent of the cases in which the department used force, it was against African Americans. In all of the 14 canine-bite incidents for which racial information was available, the person bitten was African American.

In Ferguson court cases, African Americans are 68 percent less likely than others to have their cases dismissed by a municipal judge, according to the Justice review. In 2013, African Americans accounted for 92 percent of the cases in which an arrest warrant was issued.[2]

On July 17, 2014, New York City police officers moved to arrest Eric Garner on the charge of selling loose cigarettes. Garner balked at what he felt was harassment. Several officers grabbed him and threw him to the ground. His head was pushed against the pavement as his arms were yanked backward so he could be handcuffed. "I can't breathe," he said a total of eleven times.

When Garner tied his shoes earlier that morning, how could he know that he would not live to untie them that evening? How much was his life worth? He died due to the accusation that he was selling unlicensed cigarettes.

December 3, 2015, was a chilly night in San Francisco. I stared out of the window of the T train as it passed through a part of the city that tourists would be surprised to know even existed. It is a forgotten corner of one of America's most famous vacation destinations. It is called Bayview-Hunter's Point. It is the 'hood. When I disembarked from the train, I was lost. Although I've lived in the San Francisco Bay Area for years, I was unfamiliar with this community.

It was about 7 p.m., and people flitted back and forth, heads down, no one catching eye contact. I waved at a young man who did not have the look of caution in his eyes. "Say, young man," I asked. "Can you show me where the brother fell in these streets?" He nodded and pointed to a sliver of sidewalk behind a busy boulevard. I thanked him.

There, I found taped to a tree a picture of a young black man in a woolen cap. Beneath it, surrounded by a bank of candles, was a piece of corrugated cardboard with the words, "Shame on SFPD. Mario Woods Did Not Have to Be Executed."

As in so many instances, the video evidence was clear. Five police officers followed Woods up the sidewalk. Woods was carrying a knife. At no time did any of the trained and heavily armed police officers seem to be in danger of injury. Still, they pumped fifteen bullets into his body. As in the other two cases previously mentioned, no one was charged. No one went to jail. No one even paid the fine they would incur if they shot a stray dog beneath the freeway.

THE DISPARITY IN POLICE TREATMENT

Even with substantial evidence to the contrary, many people do not believe that police misconduct is a frequent occurrence in communities of color across America. Not long ago a Christian minister wrote to me and said that a Harvard study informed him that these cases were overstated and overblown. He believes that black people play the victim role and seek preferential treatment. He does not believe that racial prejudice is still a reality in the post-Barack Obama era, especially as pertaining to law enforcement. Is the disparity in police treatment an urban myth?

In 2017 the Oakland Police Department requested a study on that particular topic due to the statistical data informing the department that there was a wide disparity between how many blacks and whites were stopped and how they were treated by police. After analyzing more than one hundred hours of body-camera footage, researchers found that blacks were 61 percent more likely to be referred to by terms like *bro* or *dude* and ordered to grab the steering wheel. Fifty-seven percent of whites were more likely to hear an apology or the words *thank you*.[3]

Blacks *are* stopped at much higher rates than whites. Police brutality is real and can happen just about anywhere to a person of color. In an article titled "Racial Gap in U.S. Arrest Rates: 'Staggering Disparity,'" *USA Today* correspondent Brad Heath writes, "At least 70 departments scattered from Connecticut to California arrested black people at a rate 10 times higher than people who are not black. . . . More than half of the people Dearborn police arrested in 2011 and 2012 were black, according to reports they submitted to the FBI. By comparison, about 4% of the city's residents are black."[4]

FBI data reveals that black people accounted for 31 percent of police killings in 2012, even though they make up only 13 percent of the population.[5]

TEARS THAT NEVER DRY

As a minister in the inner city, I have grown quite close to many people I would never have met had misfortune not struck their families. If you ever minister in the 'hood, you'll meet them as well. Some of my friends have lost loved ones to police bullets. What will you do when they tell you their stories? Not everything can be healed with a three-point sermon and some anointing oil.

These people are dealing with wounds that will never completely heal. I will introduce you to three of them.

He's my brother. Tawanda Jones is an educator in Baltimore. When her brother obtained a part-time job setting up office cubicles, she was concerned about him taking the public bus. One day she surprised him with the keys to her new Mercedes Benz. The plan was that he would drive her to work each morning, go to his own job, and then come back to pick her up on his way home. The arrangement worked well. Her bother, Tyrone West, kept the car washed and in immaculate condition. He was responsible and timely.[6]

Forty-four-year-old Tyrone was a benevolent soul who would do anything for a friend. One evening he called Tawanda and said that a young lady friend needed a ride. He asked to borrow her Mercedes, promising to bring it right back home after the favor had been performed. When he didn't return in a reasonable span of time, his sister began to worry.

That night, a sudden pain ripped through her side causing her to collapse to the floor in agony. Looking back, she believes it was a sign from God; somehow a mystical connection to her blood brother had been severed. When the pain subsided, her first thought was to reach out to him.

Tyrone failed to answer his cell phone. Her feelings of anxiety deepened. Tawanda tried again and again. Still nothing. Next, she called anyone who might know of Tyrone's location. She found the phone number of the young woman her brother was giving a ride. She did not answer the call.

Then Tawanda told her fiancé that she believed something awful had happened to Tyrone. He said he thought she was overreacting. He walked into the bedroom to watch TV. Minutes later, he got up and walked back into the living room where Tawanda was seated. He said, "I feel bad. You was right."

Tawanda asked, "Right about what?"

"They killed your brother."

Tawanda recalls, "I told him, 'Don't joke with me like that! Please don't play with me like that!' And just like that, my whole world came crashing down. I told him, 'You're making this up!'"

She said, "I turned toward the television set. I remember seeing my brother's dead body on the gurney. I saw people sobbing. The thing that touched my heart was hearing a witness say, 'I don't know why they killed that man. He was unarmed, and for them to be around him kicking him . . . '"

Tawanda said, "As he was set upon by the police, a witness said my brother was screaming, 'Trayvon Martin, help! Trayvon Martin, help!'"

"And all I could think about was our last conversation, and I could visualize him crying and screaming out another victim's name."

That night, Tawanda and several family members rushed to the police department. They wanted more information. They wanted to see Tyrone's body. They were rebuffed at every turn. First, the police refused to share any information about the slaying, even verification that Tyrone was indeed dead. Then, they told the family that someone with a medical issue had died in custody. They were calling the person John Doe. The family was told to leave and come back the next day.

We have to fight back. When I interviewed Tawanda for this book, she said, "The next day after they killed my brother, I said to myself, *We are not going to be one of those families who just put* *on a T-shirt and wait on anybody. We are going to organize.* My whole entire family stayed up for twenty-four hours. And when them detectives walked in there with their lies, we got organized real fast. We said, 'No, we're going to start going down there demanding answers.'

"Our first stop was to the state attorney's office. I will never forget. We went there demanding that they would talk to us, demanding that they would give us an account for what's happened. We wanted to know where the video footage was."

The cover-up. The police said that Tyrone, a healthy man who has just passed a company physical with flying colors, died of a heart attack due to the heat. Witnesses told another story. Tawanda recounts,

> The next day we went to the area where my brother had been killed and handed out business cards with our lawyer's phone number. Not only were there eyewitnesses, people had said they'd taken cell phone footage. When we were knocking on doors handing out our lawyer's cards, the people said, basically, "The commissioner took our cell phones and videos and said they need it for their investigation." To this day we don't have no video footage. To this day we don't have no autopsy pictures. They are really trying to hide what they did to my brother when they executed him.

West Wednesdays. The West family decided to create a community action that would bring attention to the police department's murder of their loved one. The weekly event was an outdoor protest of Tyrone's murder and a call for justice. A local pastor, Rev. C. D. Witherspoon, dubbed the gatherings "West Wednesdays."

Rain or shine, till this very day they stand on the corner and protest police violence in Baltimore. Tawanda said, "I had somebody from the NAACP tell me, 'It's cool to be out there, but y'all ain't got to be out there like that all the time for no reason, and if I'm going to come out there and be with you, it's got to be more than that.'"

I [Tawanda] said, "The reason is my brother was brutally murdered. The reason is, it's bigger than my brother. It didn't start with my brother and the sad, tragic part is, it don't end with my brother. The reason is, it's called holding people accountable. When they killed my brother and they killing others, those people don't think about the weather. They don't care if it's hot outside or if it's freezing. And I don't care about weather. When it comes down to it, I will suit up, whatever I got to do, I'm going to be out there. And that's how it's been."

After 154 consecutive West Wednesdays, the police sent word that Tyrone West had died of a heart attack due to dehydration. His family says he was tortured to death. It seems like a case of one word against another. There was only one way that one side could be proven right and the other wrong—Tyrone's body would have to be exhumed and reexamined. Tawanda and her family decided to go the length for justice. They paid $26,000 to have Tyrone's body dug up and brought back from the grave. Finally, there would be truth.

In July 2017, the city of Baltimore agreed to settle the wrongful death case of Tyrone West for one million dollars. Tawanda Jones withdrew from the case, because it included a nondefamation clause that would have stopped her from being able to speak out against her brother's murder. However, Tyrone's children will be provided for. Would any of that have happened if the West family had accepted the initial police "findings" and decided to simply go on with their lives?

A beloved son is snatched away. There is a loose-knit fellowship of families who have lost loved ones to violence in the San Francisco/Oakland Bay Area. I often see Rick Perez at such gatherings. He agreed to be interviewed for this book.[7]

Rick said,

> They pounded on the door at 4:20 in the morning on September 14, 2014. We thought they were looking for my nephew. He sometimes used our address. I opened the door to find the district attorney, the assistant district attorney, and a Richmond Police Department sergeant. I let them in. They sat down. They proceeded to ask a bunch of questions about our relationship with our son. I told them that it was good. I worked with him every day. It was a regular relationship. They asked, "When was the last time you talked to him?"
>
> I said, "You guys are asking so many questions I feel like I need a lawyer." . . . Finally, I asked straight up, "Is my son still alive?"
>
> One of them said, "I'm sorry to inform you . . ."
>
> I said, "This interview is over. You need to leave."

When the officers pressed with more questions, Rick's voice rose several decibels. "Get the f— out of my house, now!" He said. When they still hesitated, Rick began chest butting them.

After they left, Rick recalls, "I sat here and held my wife for ten minutes."

The officer had claimed that during an altercation at a local candy store, an intoxicated Pedie Perez went for a Richmond police officer's gun. This account was disputed by several eyewitnesses. According to Rick, his son Pedie was unarmed. He was trying to walk away from the officer. The officer escalated the situation. He pulled his gun. He didn't wait for backup. At the same time, Pedie called 911 to complain that the officer was harassing him. Twenty-three seconds later, he was gone. Imagine this, the message center got a call about a policeman harassing a citizen. Pedie had thirteen seconds left. The officer twisted his arm around his back and shot him.

In the aftermath of the slaying, the officer, who was thirty-three at the time, received industrial disability retirement, entitling him to $70,770 a year, tax free. Twenty-four-year-old Pedie Perez Jr., on the other hand, would never come home again. According to Rick Perez, "There was a cover-up by the Richmond Police Department. They are not acknowledging discrepancies. There was no de-escalation. He didn't call for backup. He was harassing my son."

What did Rick learn from the entire ordeal? "The police don't always tell the truth. All I want out of the whole situation is the truth."

A mother has a message for the faith community. I asked Ms. Jeralynn Brown-Blueford what it felt like when she first got word that her seventeen-year-old son Alan Blueford had been shot to death by an Oakland police officer. She said,

It was a tremendous, indescribable pain. It is like someone ripping your heart out of your chest without an incision.

There is disbelief, anger, frustration, depression, anxiety, and suicidal thoughts. When you love someone the way I loved my son, it's unimaginable to think about going on without him. I come from a praying family. If it wasn't for God, I would have gone out of my mind.

If you should find yourself in a place where a loved one has been murdered by the police, don't just take the official story, seek the truth for yourself. Never stop asking questions. Justice is deaf, dumb, and blind. It'll turn its head and act and like it doesn't understand you. It'll close its mouth and act mute. It'll cover its ears and pretend that it can't hear you. The old saying is true: too often justice means "just us."[8]

From the beginning, Ms. Brown-Blueford doubted the official account of her son's demise. She obtained the services of a lawyer and then began canvassing the neighborhood door-to-door for witnesses. She met with the police chief and other city officials who all stuck by the official version of events. They said that Alan was murdered while threatening a police officer with a gun.

The officer who murdered Alan Blueford came to Oakland with a colorful backstory. When he served as a police office in New York City, he and three other officers were the subjects of a civil rights lawsuit. It was alleged that they had beaten and maced a man confined to a jail cell. Witnesses to the shooting of young Alan Blueford said he posed no threat to the officer. Eventually, the city of Oakland agreed to a cash payout in civil court. The officer who ended Alan's life left town under a cloud. Eventually, he re-appeared as the alleged protagonist in a police abuse case when hired as a police officer in another California town.

ARE ALL POLICE OFFICERS EVIL?

In the aftermath of the Mario Woods killing in San Francisco, I went to San Francisco City Hall to sit in on a city council hearing about the matter. Thousands of people had the same idea that night. We were angry and loud. A phalanx of helmeted police in riot gear lined the front of the great, stone city hall building. I was walking past the line of law enforcement officers to enter the building when a voice called my name. I turned to my right. The voice had come from the police line. Yes, it came from one of the officers. I stared through the glass of his riot helmet. It's a good thing I don't have heart disease; my life would have ended right then. The eyes staring back at me belonged to a member of the church I was attending. They belonged to a friendly family man who went out of his way to show me hospitality each Sunday. I didn't even know he was a police officer. And there he was, staring at me through his helmet shield. Are all police officers evil? No. Not by a long shot. Not that man. Still—he represents something.

The police are the frontline soldiers for a system that has been arrayed against people of color since Christopher Columbus first shook hands with the Native Americans. When those flashing red lights and sirens race past ghetto street corners, they represent bloody backroom confessions, sons and fathers who took a one-way trip to court and never came home, fees, fines, impounded cars, parole, probation, and a million trials without a peer in sight. Police uniforms represent tears, incarceration, and death.

In Oakland, where I live, there is a coffee shop that refuses service to police officers in uniform, probably for all of the above reasons. The Oakland Police Department has existed under the oversight of the federal government for years due to tales of intimidation, abuse, and murder. However, at the end of the day, the issue is not good cops or bad cops. It's about the machine behind it all.

PRISON INDUSTRIAL COMPLEX

In the award-winning book *Ghetto: The Invention of a Place, the History of an Idea*, Mitchell Duneier informs readers that hundreds of years ago European ghettos were originally enclosed residential spaces where Jewish people were confined. Musing about the term *ghetto* in the twenty-first century, Duneier says,

> We are left with the remnants of an age-old system of exclusion—and no straightforward remedy. Worse yet, we are not emerging from what has arguably been the largest and most consequential of all interventions in the lives of poor blacks, a war on drugs based ultimately on its own misguided fantasy of a solution. The tactic emerged gradually only after deindustrialization rendered poor urban blacks increasingly superfluous. The ghetto became a hyperpoliced and monitored zone. Today, most of the men in the ghetto, subject as they are to paramilitary-style policing such as stop and frisk operations, will spend some time in prison. The ghetto can no longer be defined as a segregated area in which poor blacks live. It is better understood as a place of intrusive social control for poor blacks.[9]

Hyperpolicing and mass incarceration are at the root of the social control of which Duneier speaks so eloquently.

The United States of America incarcerates more people than any nation in history. It locks up more people than China and Russia together. In the book *Prison Industrial Complex for Beginners*, author James Braxton Peterson writes, "The United States does not lead the world in quality of public education, access to health care, life expectancy, or many of the other social metrics that matter to its citizens. Do we as a nation want to be number one incarcerator in the world?"[10]

I would encourage every reader to study the Sentencing Project website (sentencingproject.org). Click on "Racial Disparity" and discover that on any given day in America, one out of every ten black men in his thirties is either in prison or jail. There are many reasons for this malady. The first might be the ill-fated War on Drugs, which was launched by Richard Nixon and escalated under the Ronald Reagan administration. Law enforcement targeted communities populated by people of color. Draconian penalties were given to people of color found selling even miniscule amounts of crack, whereas those found with comparative amounts of powder cocaine (more than likely in white suburbs) were given lighter sentences.

The notorious plea bargaining setup is the justice system's biggest trap. Let's say you are arrested. Whether you're guilty or innocent doesn't really matter in this arena. Yes, we all know that you have a right to a fair and speedy trial. (At least that's what it says in the Constitution.) However, poor people who can't afford bail are kept locked up indefinitely. Eventually, the district attorney's office offers you a deal: forgo your right to a trial and take this plea bargain. If you don't and you lose in a court trial, you will be buried for years. Besides, the system is laced with snitches, people who will say you did it even though they have never seen you before; it's their ticket out of jail. By the time you get out of prison, your kids might not even remember you.

Racial minorities are more likely than white Americans to be arrested; once arrested, they are more likely to be convicted; and once convicted, they are more likely to face stiff sentences. African-American males are six times more likely to be incarcerated than white males and 2.5 times more likely than Hispanic males. If current trends continue, one of every three black American males born today can expect to go to prison in his lifetime, as can one of every six Latino males—compared to one of every seventeen white males. Racial and ethnic disparities among women are less substantial than among men but remain prevalent.[11]

The system is highly monetized. In his book *Understanding Mass Incarceration*, James Kilgore writes, "In 2012 New York spent more than $60,000 a year to incarcerate one person. By comparison, the total 2011-2012 annual cost of attending Harvard was $52,652 for tuition, room, board, and fees combined."[12]

Entire industries from food distributors to phone companies eat hardily from the devil's pie called incarceration. So lucrative is the punishment industry that California built twenty prisons in the time frame that it built one university. Facilities spring up in the middle of nowhere that must be built and staffed with highly compensated personnel. A huge number of people in prison have severe mental health problems and drug-dependency issues. Private prisons have now sprung up all over the country, and their stock is traded on Wall Street. Not everyone loses in the punishment-industry game. A large number of people are getting fat from it.

Bob Dylan once sang, "Steal a little and they throw you in jail, steal a lot and they make you king."[13] There seems to be some truth in that lyric. According to James Kilgore, "People in prison and jails have lower average incomes on the outside than the general population, are more likely to be unemployed and less likely to have completed high school or college. They represent the poorest, most marginalized members to the U.S. working class."[14]

Kilgore states that America has a two-tiered punishment system. A wealthy person who steals a great deal of money will more than likely serve much less time than a poor person who was arrested for a relatively small amount of drugs or theft.

DEVASTATING SENTENCES

One of the earmarks of the War on Drugs was harsh, inflexible sentences. Federal guidelines were put in place that forced judges to give lengthy sentences even when the punishment did not fit the crime. These stretches were known as "mandatory minimums." Some states adopted three-strikes laws. People labeled habitual criminals could be given life sentences if convicted of three "strippable" offenses. Rapper Tupac once rapped, "The three strikes law is drastic / And certain death for us ghetto bastards."[15]

Dewayne Williams caught a third strike for stealing a slice of pizza in 1995. He did five years for that slice before a judge reviewed his case and set him free. I personally met someone who caught a third strike for stealing a jacket.

Many of the people who are arrested in the 'hood have mental-health issues. People who live in places where random instances of violent crime are a way of life sometimes have trouble coping with the sudden deaths of classmates, friends, neighbors, and relatives. There are a limited number of mental-health facilities in the inner cities to treat the ill, especially those dealing with trauma. A large group of prisoners wrestles with drug addiction. Treatment is not a major emphasis behind bars. If recovery is not available for prisoners with drug problems, recidivism is almost a certainty.

If people walk in to prison totally sane, twenty-three-hour lockup in solitary confinement might challenge that. Some prison facilities don't have windows or allow human contact.

Inmates must leave their children to be raised by grandparents or the other parent. As most inmates are poor, already stretched resources are pushed to the breaking point. The incarcerated are not provided hygiene products behind bars. Family members must send those products and provide money for incidentals. Everything from phone minutes to deodorant is sold at inflated prices. It's like shopping at the airport.

Eventually, when the incarcerated are released, they remain under control of the state. They must report their whereabouts to a parole or probation officer. Fees and fines are owed to the state. Often the convicted are charged restitution that places money into the hands of the victim. In some states, prisoners are charged room and board for their prison cells, payable upon release. Prisoners in some jurisdictions are charged for electronic ankle bracelet monitoring, case filing, and drug testing. In California, the person is released with $200 in gate money. In

2012, 5.8 million people were denied the right to vote due to a felony conviction.[16]

Michelle Alexander, author of the seminal book *The New Jim Crow*, writes:

> Today, most Americans know and don't know the truth about mass incarceration. For more than three decades, images of black men in handcuffs have been a regular staple of the evening news. We know that large numbers of black men have been locked in cages. In fact, it is precisely because we know that black and brown people are far more likely to be imprisoned that we, as a nation, have not cared too much about it. We tell ourselves they "deserve" their fate, even though we know—and don't know—that whites are just as likely to commit many crimes, especially drug crimes. We know that people released from prison face a lifetime of discrimination, scorn and exclusion, and yet we claim not to know that an undercaste exists. We know and we don't know at the same time.[17]

THE CHURCH MUST ACT NOW

Let me stand outside the doors of the inner-city church and help you see what the people in the 'hood see. They see a fortune spent on maintaining a church building where they may not feel welcome. They see great sums of money spent to keep the pastor in a lifestyle worthy of that person's position and stature. They don't see anybody inside engaged in the struggle to bring down the iron house of slavery called prison. They hear a lot of Scriptures being quoted, but nothing being said about how the people of God are going to raise a fist on behalf of inner-city children.

Brothers and sisters in Christ, if we are to survive, we have to do something different. People of limited means must know that if anybody is going to stand up for them, it's us. Christians have been given the mandate. If we don't fight for the impoverished, the disenfranchised, the crushed, and the oppressed, we will completely lose the respect of the people.

In his album *Lethal Injection*, gangsta rap icon Ice Cube has a skit that precedes the song "When I Get to Heaven." As a gangsta he approaches a clueless Christian in the middle of the 'hood staring into the sky awaiting the return of Jesus. Cube says, "Damn, so you still out here waiting, huh?" The believer responds in the affirmative. As he dips his hand into the man's pockets, Ice Cube asks, "So you don't mind if I take this watch and the car keys?" The Christian responds, "No, Jesus will give me another one." Ice Cube says, "Cool," as he opens the door to the believer's newly gifted car and drives away.[18]

For Ice Cube (and plenty of young people) the church is so otherworldly in its focus that it pays little attention to issues like mass incarceration and police abuse. Like the poor caricature in the skit, we are just staring into the skies dreaming of the afterlife. Dr. King warned against this many years earlier. In an interview with *Playboy* magazine, King said,

> There are many signs that the judgment of God is upon the church as never before. Unless the early sacrificial spirit is recaptured, I am very much afraid that today's Christian church will lose its authenticity, forfeit the loyalty of millions,

and we will see the Christian church dismissed as a social club with no meaning or effectiveness for our time, as a form without substance, as salt without savor.[19]

Jesus' call to love one's neighbor and Christ's honor of the sanctity of all human lives requires us to do what we must to stand against systems and powers that would justify murder and rampant, merciless incarceration of the poor. This is the resistance.

In Job 29, the stricken man looks back over his life as a community leader and sums it like this:

> When the ear heard me, then it blessed me; and when the eye saw me, it gave witness to me: Because I delivered the poor that cried, and the fatherless, and him that had none to help him. The blessing of him that was ready to perish came upon me: and I caused the widow's heart to sing for joy. I put on righteousness, and it clothed me: my judgment was as a robe and a diadem. I was eyes to the blind, and feet was I to the lame. I was a father to the poor: and the cause which I knew not I searched out. And I brake the jaws of the wicked, and plucked the spoil out of his teeth. (Job 29:11-17 KJV)

There is so much to chew on in this passage, but verse 16 in particular bears direct correlation to our study: "I was a father to the poor: and the cause which I knew not I searched out." What role does a good father play in a home? He is the protector, is he not? And then Job says, "And the cause which I knew not I searched out."

Job helped people get to the root of things. He worked on behalf of people who were mistreated and denied justice. Community member, pastor, minister: sometimes the hardest thing to find out when someone is slain is the actual sequence of events leading to the shooting. What really happened? When the bulletin interrupts your favorite television program or the knock comes to your front door, will you be ready to help seek the truth? Talk to the person. Ask the family. More than likely, there is some way to help.

Jeremiah 31:15 says,

> This is what the LORD says:
> "A voice is heard in Ramah,
>> mourning and great weeping,
> Rachel weeping for her children
>> and refusing to be comforted,
> because they are no more."

This is the most insensitive thing you can say to someone who has lost a child to a policeman's bullet: "That's enough, now. Get over it." That person will never "get over it." It takes some people years to actually admit that the loss has occurred, let alone enter the grieving process. Some hospitals have grief circles in which people who have been wounded by loss can talk freely and without judgment. Why don't you establish such a circle in your church? Why not bring in a professional grief counselor to help people who have experienced the traumatic loss of a loved one? You could even have a church service in which people who have lost loved ones to gun violence can bring pictures of their loved ones and share stories. This could be followed by a season of prayer or embrace.

From what I have heard and learned from parents who lost children, acknowledgment of the loss can provide a measure of comfort.

QUESTIONS THAT DEMAND ANSWERS

Can you answer these questions for me: What are your legal rights when stopped by a police officer? What are you required by law to say when questioned? Under what circumstances can a police officer search you or your vehicle?

If you don't know the answers to those questions, chances are that your congregants or the people you serve don't know either. Why not host a workshop at your church that will inform your members of what they should or should not do when stopped by the police? Get a criminal defense lawyer or a public defender to share information with your members.

Have you ever been to a city hall meeting? Would you know which city official to contact if church members or neighbors knocked on your door and said that their child had been beaten by the police? Who holds the police accountable? Who would investigate a brutality complaint against an officer?

Do you have regular dialogue with the police who patrol the area where you minister? Do you know them? Would they know you if you were to make a phone call?

If you answered no to any of these questions, then you know what you need to do. Don't wait until something bad happens to one of your parishioners or one of your friends. Be proactive. Do your due diligence. Do your footwork and learn the answers to those questions. Equip your neighbors or parishioners with the information that might keep them alive or out of custody.

PLEA TO THE BELIEVERS

s. Jeralynn Brown-Blueford what the role of the faith
unity should be in journeying with members who have lost
ed ones to police violence. She said:

The church is not just behind the four walls of a building.
The church is the community. You have to pastor the
community and not just on Sunday. You've got to serve
the people and be active with the people, not just on Easter
and Christmas. You've got to be a presence among the people.

Everyone has an agenda, but Pastor, the people's agenda
is bigger than your agenda. You have to get out there and
listen to the people. Pastors don't want to make waves. That
might get in the way of their churches getting grants. They
want to be friendly with people in power who are going to
push their agenda.

Sometimes, preachers are just are reluctant to do the hard
work. My son being killed by police is an ugly thing. So
people don't want to be associated with something like that.
The preachers don't want to be subjected to or associated
with the pain and misery of an ugly thing like that, so they
hang back.

Jesus went to the ugly situations. Jesus did the hard, ugly
work. A lot of pastors don't want to do that because it makes
it difficult on so many levels.

Jesus said, "Take up your cross." It doesn't matter the
ethnicity of the group. It's the relationship with God. We
need pastors who have a love for God's people; they can get
past traditions, ethnicities, even religions.[20]

HOMEWORK

- Write a letter to one of the people in this book who lost a loved one to police violence. (Feel free to send it to the email address at the end of the book. I will forward it to them.)

- Write your thoughts about the church's connection to social justice and its role in the fight against mass incarceration.

THE RISE OF THE PROSPERITY GOSPEL

The Scriptural Interpretation That Kills

When I was in college, I used to go to a Friday morning Bible study sponsored by two older men in the community, Winston and Leonard. I so enjoyed listening to these two seasoned believers battle over nuances contained within the Scripture passages we studied.

One day, I received word that Winston was gravely ill. My heart sank. It turned out that he'd been sick for a long time but refused medical care due to his faith convictions. Whenever a sharp pain shot through his innards, Winston would quote Isaiah 53:5:

> But he was pierced for our transgressions,
>   he was crushed for our iniquities;
> the punishment that brought us peace was on him,
>   and by his wounds we are healed.

When asked the reason for his moaning and groaning, he would look at his wife and merely respond with Proverbs 18:21: "Death and life are in the power of the tongue: and they that love it shall eat the fruit thereof" (KJV).

Winston was a firm believer in the prosperity gospel. He believed that sickness was of the devil and could not lay hold on the believer. He believed that the shed blood of Jesus canceled illness. All a person had to do was believe. He also believed strongly in one of the core tenets of the prosperity gospel: words create, and we will have what we say with our lips, whether good or bad. Therefore he would never say, "I hurt" or "I'm sick." He would only say, "I am well. I am fine." Some call this the "name it and claim it gospel." He called it "positive confession." As Winston drew near death's door, his family was finally able to persuade him to go to the hospital. His doctor called for a series of tests, some of them painful. Winston refused any medicine to dull the discomfort, again standing on his understanding of the Scriptures on healing. According to the results, Winston's body was wracked with disease. However, he refused to accept the doctor's diagnosis. He went to his early grave quoting Scripture out of context. The pastor who indoctrinated my late friend with that faulty theology was as guilty as a hit man who places his gun up against the head of his victim and pulls the trigger for money.

Often, the excesses of the prosperity gospel are laughed at, but I assure you that this is no laughing matter. People have been bankrupted. Folks have had their faith stolen from them. And in cases like Winston's, people have lost their lives. That's why any resistance movement must warn the innocent and the unsuspecting about this false gospel. The preachers of the prosperity gospel are assassins of the gospel of hope and empowerment. They use false hope instead of bullets.

DADDY GRACE AND THE UNITED HOUSE OF PRAYER

I could write a fascinating book about Christian preachers who live in villas, own fleets of luxury cars, and have amassed private fortunes through the misinterpretation of that one single verse (Isaiah 53:5). These preachers have driven many away and made skeptics of would-be believers. But they are a colorful lot. Let me tell you about one of the early prosperity preachers.

At the height of the Great Depression, Daddy Grace was weighed down in studded diamonds and sapphires. His fingernails were three inches long. Decades before men wore long hair as a fashion statement, his white locks flowed down over his suit jacket collar. Born Marcelino Manuel da Graça, he considered himself of "White Portuguese" ethnicity. He did not see himself as African American and said openly that no African American could do what he was doing. And he was doing it! By 1953, Graça's church owned real estate holdings in both the United States and Cuba, including the Eldorado Hotel on Central Park West, which was rumored to be worth eighteen million dollars in 1953.

Though the pastor of the United House of Prayer claimed to be a poor man, he owned a fleet of expensive automobiles and wore tailor-made suits, hand-painted neckties, and expensive jewelry.

Daddy, as he was called, would walk through the doors only after service was in full swing. His followers would throw flower petals down in his path. People tried to touch him. When he sat on the "holy throne," female followers fanned his brow. It was said that he would sit there thumbing through registered letters containing cash donations.

The most important part of the service was taking the offering. A shout band and concert band provided the raucous music for flag carriers and majorettes. There was a service almost every night. On Saturday night, services lasted so long that people simply slept in the church and waited for Sunday school. Financial collections were taken in aluminum pans by men who struggled to outdo one another; the one collecting the largest sum was promised a seat next to Daddy Grace himself during the church service. "Please put something in *my* pan!" "Please swell *my* total!" they hollered. Grace preferred paper bills: "The sound of metal hurts my ears," said the spiritual leader.[1]

Baptism was certainly unusual at the United House of Prayer. It was held outdoors, and the water was provided by a local firefighter's hose.

> As Grace raised his hands, with fingernails from one to three inches, and fingers graced with diamonds and sapphires, local firemen turned on the hose. As soon as the water struck them, the converts began dancing, shivering, twisting, prancing. . . . They screamed into the water, praising the sweet name of Daddy while Daddy stood safely under an umbrella and said, "Ain't I pretty?"[2]

The overwhelming majority of Daddy Grace's followers lacked formal education. Often, they were poor people rejected by upwardly mobile, middle-class churches pastored by educated ministers. They were earnest souls attracted to a man who threw out strands of Scripture like lifelines in a turbulent world. However, in the years following Grace's reign, a bevy of preachers borrowed his zest for making money and mixed it with Scripture. These evangelists drew not only the uneducated but those with advanced degrees. A Daddy Grace church service was an event.

DADDY GRACE'S THEOLOGY

Did Daddy Grace believe that he was God? Apparently, the role of an almighty deity wasn't enough for the pastor. "Never mind about God," he was once quoted as saying. "Salvation is by Grace only. . . . Grace has given God a vacation, and since God is on His vacation, don't worry about Him. . . . If you sin against God, Grace can save you, but if you sin against Grace, God cannot save you."[3]

One of his followers once prayed,

> Heavenly Father, we thank thee for Daddy. We thank thee for sending him into the world at this critical hour to lead us from darkness to light. For when we were lost as wandering sheep, Daddy came upon the scene and saved our souls. And we know for a truth that today Daddy holds the entire world in the hollow of his hand. We know that if we only trust in Daddy everything will be alright. Even from the beginning of time our sweet Daddy had us in his mind. We know that we have found the true way at last that we shall be saved, O Heavenly Father, for thou said in thy holy word that by Grace are ye saved.[4]

Here's the testimony of another follower:

> I died, fell dead in the doorway. But Daddy Grace put his hand on my chest and right away it was like an electric shock passing through me. . . . There isn't any leader except Grace. There isn't any religion except through Grace. Grace can heal you. When he puts the Grace Magazine on your chest, it is the healing power of spirit. . . . Grace is the greatest thing in the world. Grace will bring you through.[5]

Besides healing, Sweet Daddy Grace was a master at branding. The faith healer sold his own cookies, creams, powders, shoe polish soap, toothpaste, and even coffee. He died a wealthy man.

SWEET DADDY'S CHILDREN

Daddy Grace spawned many imitators. There are many who have taken threads of his "gospel" and woven them together into a message that would bring them personal acclaim—and everything from private jets to a $24,000 toilet seat.

Some years ago, a well-known "prophetess" was featured at a church I attended. I wasn't there that night, but I received the report from friends who had participated in the service. After the last notes of praise and worship had evaporated into the ether, she received an offering from business owners who wanted Almighty God to cause their enterprises to thrive. According to the prophetess, God's blessings were going for $100 a pop that night. The question was, did the attendees have enough faith to sacrifice? Were they there to simply "tip" God, or did they have the faith to grasp a miracle?

On cue, unsmiling ushers passed baskets on all three levels of the massive sanctuary. They seemed to be counting the take with their eyes. Wallets flipped open. Purses clicked open. According to the renowned speaker, God was watching now. Her voice was so thunderous and commanding. Who could doubt her? Thousands began to fill the coffers.

The people continued to sacrifice as the prophetess lifted up the second verse of "Amazing Grace." She broke into a holy version of "Peppermint Twist" and lifted her eyes toward heaven or at least the top row where an usher was shaking a basket impatiently in front of a senior citizen in a tattered gray raincoat.

A woman sitting in the third row on the second level wavered. Perhaps she was trying to decide whether to "step out in faith" or play it safe and pay the gas and electric bill. Faith won over. However, the ushers had already begun to make their way back to the front of the auditorium with the baskets brimming with money. The eagle-eyed prophet noticed the hundred-dollar bill being waved in the back of the room. She called out to the woman, "Uh-uh! The Holy Ghost says, 'Tax.'" The giver was penalized another $100 because she had hesitated when God spoke. With a grim expression on her face, she reached back into her worn leather purse to retrieve it. Of course, some of the second hundred was made of one-dollar bills and quarters the woman had set aside for laundry. The prophet graciously accepted all of it.

A couple of years ago, TV cameras gave us a grand tour of a sprawling, palatial estate, complete with a dining room that resembled the set of the feature film *King Arthur and the Knights of the Round Table*. With the aid of Scripture the owner, a preacher sitting by the Olympic-size swimming pool, explained his mansion, his $300,000 Rolls Royce, and his generous salary. He quoted 3 John 1:2, which says, "Beloved, I wish above all things that thou mayest prosper and be in health, even as thy soul prospereth" (KJV).

That Scripture is the cornerstone of what is often called the "prosperity gospel." *Prosperity* is a powerful word. Dictionary.com tells us that its primary meaning is "a successful, flourishing, or thriving condition, especially in financial respects; good fortune." Secondarily it means "Characterized by financial success or good fortune."

Reading those definitions into that isolated text would certainly seem to justify God's will for the popular evangelist to amass great wealth at the expense of his followers. This man has built a theology and a ministry from those few words. But does 3 John 1:2 actually mean that God wishes the Christian financial prosperity above all things?

The word *prosperity* has tripped us up. In his commentary, theologian John Painter translates the passage: "Beloved, I desire that all may go well with you and that you may enjoy good health even as I know it is well with your soul."[6] The New Revised Standard Version of the Bible says basically the same thing.

John is writing to Gaius, a faithful servant of Jesus Christ. The apostle opens the letter with a good health wish, which was typical for a Greek letter. Today, it might be akin to opening a letter with the words "I hope this letter finds you well." *Prosper* would be better translated "to fare well." The quote ends with a prayer for spiritual well-being. We'd be hard-pressed to find a legitimate biblical scholar who would translate that passage to mean prayer for increased financial and material wealth. It's just not there. The preacher who has bilked millions of dollars out of his poor congregants to buy his mansion and his fleet of luxury cars is in error if he uses that Scripture as his basis for the right to great wealth.

Yet there are many preachers who have amassed private fortunes through misinterpreting Scripture.

SUFFERING IS PART OF THE FAITH EXPERIENCE

Using 3 John 1:2 as a proof text, prosperity preachers tell their followers that good health is the divine right of the believer.

In his book *The Problem of Pain*, C. S. Lewis wrote,

What would really satisfy us would be a God who said of anything we happened to like doing, "What does it matter so long as they are contented?" We want, in fact, not so much a Father in Heaven as a grandfather in heaven—a senile benevolence who, as they say, "liked to see young people enjoying themselves," and whose plan for the universe was simply that it might be truly said at the end of each day, "a good time was had by all."[7]

But can suffering be avoided by quoting Scripture and maintaining a positive confession in the face of trouble? Is God's plan for our life to be an existence free from distress or pain, a life in which prosperity and good health are our birthrights because of our relationship with God?

The wealthy landowner's prosperity. Luke 12:13-21 tells the story of a wealthy landowner who received an unexpected windfall. He mulls over his plans for the extra blessing: "This is what I'll do. I will tear down my barns and build bigger ones, and there I will store my surplus grain. And I'll say to myself, 'You have plenty of grain laid up for many years. Take life easy; eat, drink and be merry'" (vv. 18-19).

The story doesn't end well. God calls him a fool and announces that he will not live to see the morning. His blessing might well have come from God, but his view of what to do with it was skewed.

Skip Moen, a biblical scholar, was one of my undergraduate philosophy professors at Sean University in Union, New Jersey. In a recent conversation he said,

In the Hebrew language there is no word for possessions: things which belong exclusively to me. There is always the obligation for a communal response to need. The wealthy are obligated to share God's provision. All of your material things are on loan from God for the benefit of the others. As soon as you stop being a conduit, you are in violation of God's laws. God's plan centers on distribution, not accumulation.

In this story, God has provided so much that the rich man should have distributed it to others, not hoarded. Relationship with God necessitates that we are givers. Pay it forward. It flows through you to others.[8]

Job disrupts the prosperity principle. In the first chapter of the book of Job, messengers arrive at Job's front door, one shortly after the other, each with bad news. The first messenger informs Job that a marauding party has made off with Job's donkeys and oxen, which were worth a fortune. The second messenger arrives with news that all of Job's servants have been slaughtered, except the one standing before him. A third messenger tells Job that a mighty wind has just destroyed the house where his children were celebrating. All ten of them died in the disaster. By the time the third messenger has gone his way, Job's entire life has been flipped upside down.

Job did not plead for God to recall his promises of wealth. He said simply:

> Naked I came from my mother's womb,
>   and naked I will depart.
> The Lord gave and the Lord has taken away;
>   may the name of the Lord be praised. (Job 1:21)

In Job 2:7, we find Satan afflicting Job with painful boils. As the story goes on, his situation becomes so dire that his wife suggests that he curse God and die (Job 2:9). Yes, God restores Job's material wealth and heals him, but there is one thing that cannot be overlooked. Job's ten children will never return to him. Even with additional family members added to his clan, he will still weep for those ten for the rest of his days.

As the story ends, we realize that Job is a pawn in a contest between God and Satan. Job never finds that out. His suffering is a testament for the ages. God used his pain to teach others. Is it possible that God can do the same thing with us if God so chooses?

The rich young ruler and prosperity. In Mark 10, Jesus is going about his way when a young fellow falls at Jesus' feet and asks the existential question of the ages, "Good Teacher, what must I do to inherit eternal life?"(v. 17). Jesus tells him to keep the commandments. The young man says that he has done so since he was young, but it seems that something is yet lacking. "Jesus looked at him and loved him. 'One thing you lack,' he said, 'Go, sell everything you have and give to the poor, and you will have treasure in heaven. Then come, follow me'" (v. 21).

Uh-oh! The young man was not expecting this three-point answer. Jesus tells him to sell everything he possesses. Second, he is to give the proceeds to the poor. Third, after he has divested he is told to follow Jesus, being promised riches in heaven.

This is the opposite of prosperity preaching!

When the man walks away sorrowful, unwilling to depart with his possessions, Jesus shares a teaching with his disciples that raises eyebrows. "Jesus looked around and said to his disciples, 'How hard it is for the rich to enter the kingdom of God! . . . It is easier for a camel to go through the eye of a needle than for someone who is rich to enter the kingdom of God.' The disciples were even more amazed" (Mark 10:23-26).

The faithful and prosperity. Hebrews 11 is often called the "Faith Hall of Fame." The writer lists some of God's most faithful servants. He says, in part,

> Women received back their dead, raised to life again. There were others who were tortured, refusing to be released so that they might gain an even better resurrection. Some faced jeers and flogging, and even chains and imprisonment. They were put to death by stoning; they were sawed in two; they were killed by the sword. They went about in sheepskins and goatskins, destitute, persecuted and mistreated—the world was not worthy of them. They wandered in deserts and mountains, living in caves and in holes in the ground.
>
> These were all commended for their faith, yet none of them received what had been promised, since God had planned something better for us so that only together with us would they be made perfect. (Hebrews 11:35-40)

Is the prosperity gospel in line with the spirit and tenor of the Scriptures? It would seem to me that if God's will for all believers is prosperity, Jesus himself would have been quite wealthy. Instead, Jesus says, "Foxes have dens and birds have nests, but the Son of Man has no place to lay his head" (Matthew 8:20). That is the textbook definition of homelessness.

THE PROSPERITY GOSPEL AND THE POOR

Prosperity gospel churches do not have a strong social justice presence in their communities. The prosperity gospel is not a community-empowerment message. It is a recipe for personal enrichment. Its goals are largely at odds with ministries that strive for social justice. To check the veracity of this, visit the websites of America's most successful prosperity preachers. They have testimonies of people who benefited from their ministry. Almost all of those testimonies will have an *I, me,* and *my* bent to them. Try to find one that says, "I sowed $1,000 into Prophet X's ministry and then two weeks later the city built a children's hospital on my side of town that they are now naming after the man of God."

Write to me the day you find one that says, "Evangelist A laid hands on our police chief and claims of police brutality were cut in half within six months." Basically, it doesn't work that way. Sowing a seed is a personal investment plan that God's name gets attached to, but for many, the slot machine never pays off.

Most of the "name it and claim it" gospel rests on two fallacies. The first is interpreting the Bible in a manner that is not true to the original meaning assigned to it by those who wrote it. Biblical scholars often say, "The Bible can never mean what it never meant." It is wrong to cherry-pick verses out of context and fuse them together to support a view that is different from what the writers originally meant.

For example, let's look at Galatians 6:7-10:

Do not be deceived: God cannot be mocked. A man reaps what he sows. Whoever sows to please their flesh, from the flesh will reap destruction; whoever sows to please the Spirit, from the Spirit will reap eternal life. Let us not become weary in doing good, for at the proper time we will reap a harvest if we do not give up. Therefore, as we have opportunity, let us do good to all people, especially to those who belong to the family of believers.

When trying to prove that God has promised to give money to those who give to their ministries, prosperity preachers often remove the first sentence of this passage. Yes, it clearly says, "a man reaps what he sows." However, look closely at the words surrounding that sentence (its context). Paul talks about sowing to the flesh and the spirit. The harvest he goes on to talk about reaping is a spiritual one. Look at the true spirit of the text. Is Paul saying that if you do good to people within the church body, you will harvest a financial reward? Yes, it is within God's power to give, but we would be hard-pressed to show where this passage provides support for a biblical financial investment and return principle. It just isn't there.

The second fallacy is idolatry. At the helm of many prosperity ministries is a charismatic leader who would give the devil a run for his money. This person is a gifted persuader wearing expensive clothing. The message is: "Yes, believe the Bible, but if you can't find what I say in the Bible, believe me."

Everyone loves a winner, right? Many of the leader's followers are drawn to the expensive clothing, the high-profile friends, and the opulent buildings. Does connection to such affluence produce joy? Not for the bivocational preacher who shows up at church after closing his plumbing shop.

These larger-than-life figures persuade normal, levelheaded people to choose that which defies common sense. The prosperity preachers use their near-hypnotic abilities to encourage us to remove money from our family's food and utility budget for their

Hawaiian cruises. Then we sit around the kitchen table in the cold and dark because we put our electric bill money in their offering basket. Our children complain that their bellies are empty, and we think, *There is one consolation: at least Rev. So-and-So will be able to sip on Dom Pérignon champagne while he's cruising to Oahu!*

These hustling charlatans make their bread and butter off of the poorest of the poor. They have every senior in the trailer park or the housing project on a mailing list. So if you serve Christ in the 'hood, it won't be long before you run into this doctrine. But don't make the person being conned feel foolish. Don't downgrade Prophet Makeasuckerouttayou. Lead the person you're discipling to the Ten Commandments and read the second one out loud. Discuss it thoroughly. What is idolatry? How do you define it? Is it confined to golden calves and images of Baal, or could it mean a human being we worship like Jesus?

MIND CONTROL: THE GREATEST DANGER

Jim Jones was a brilliant communicator with a vision that resonated in the hearts of many good-hearted and intelligent people. Jones believed in a nonracial society. He didn't just preach this concept; he lived it. Jones and his wife, Marceline, were the first white couple in the history of Indiana to adopt a black child. He crusaded against racial intolerance long before the civil rights movement took on steam. This appealed not only to blacks who had seen racism at its ugliest but to a great number of white people as well. Much to the chagrin of local churchgoers, Jones sometimes led his multiracial following into segregated church services, which created raucous disturbances.

Preacher Jones adopted many of the trappings of the black church experience—the preaching cadence, the ecstatic worship. Jones even performed "miracles." He eventually renounced the Bible's authority. However, a few Scriptures suited him. One of them was Acts 4:32: "All the believers were one in heart and mind. No one claimed that any of their possessions was their own, but they shared everything they had." He cajoled members into leaving their homes, sometimes selling their properties and giving the money to the People's Temple, Jones's church. Followers signed over paychecks, pensions, stocks, bonds, jewelry, and social security benefits to the church. In turn they were taken care of. They lived communally.

Jones took more from his followers than their money. He used their bodies, both men's and women's. Of course, he claimed that this was for their own good and he derived no pleasure from it. Jones separated families, taking one family's children and ordering them to live with another family. He encouraged tattling. People who broke his rules were publicly shamed, even beaten before the group. What was worse, they were made to exact physical punishment on their own children based on someone else's word. Adherents to the faith were asked to throw away family pictures and mementos from their old lives.

During one spirited church service, Jones told his followers, "You prayed to your sky God, and he never heard your prayers. You asked and begged and pleaded in your suffering, and he never gave you any food. He never gave you a bed, and he never provided a home. But I, *your socialist worker god*, have given you all of these things." Jaws dropped. Jones had tiptoed toward the edge of blasphemy. Now, he crossed the line. He picked up his big, black Bible and hurled it to the floor. "You won't die if you stand on it." And then he did just that, his toes hanging off the edge of the Bible. "When your world has failed you, I'll be standing. . . . Because I am freedom," he cried out. "I am peace. I am justice. . . . I AM GOD!!!!" The crowd was persuaded. A roar of approval swept through the room.[9]

The People's Temple housed the homeless. It clothed the naked. It freed the prisoners. It fed the hungry and worked to build a world of racial equality and inclusion when many churches did not see those actions as necessities. Perhaps that is why so many of its members were willing to turn a blind eye to so many of the things that were unquestionably false and wrong. Plus, there was "Dad" (Jones). Oh, how they trusted him! When he offered to be their savior and their god, many took him up on that.

In 1978, nearly a thousand people flew to the jungles of Guyana, South America, with Jones to build a compound where their utopia of a nonracial paradise could become a reality. When a US congressman flew to investigate complaints lodged by family members back in the United States, Jones realized that the lid would soon be blown off and tales of torture and depravation would become known to the world. Jonestown's days were numbered. After Jones told the people it was time to die, one elderly man stepped up to the microphone weeping and said, "Dad, we're all ready to go. If you tell us we have to give our lives now, we're ready—I'm pretty sure all the rest of the sisters and brothers are with me."[10]

At Jones's command, 918 people drank Kool-Aid laced with poison. Many of them are buried in a graveyard that is within walking distance of my apartment building. Here in the Bay Area, the reverberations of the Jonestown massacre still echo. I have met a number of people who were members of the People's Temple. I have spoken with a number of people who knew Jones himself. None of these people are mentally disturbed. They are neither gullible nor weak minded. For a great deal of those who counted themselves as followers, no one ever sat down and taught them the true principles of the Christian faith. Sharing in these principles, these rightly divided words of truth, is foundational to the resistance.

THE TRUTH SHALL SET YOU FREE

The Word of God is the only cure for heresy. However, the teacher of God's Word must understand the correct rules of interpretation. Removing Scripture from one context and fusing it to words from another context will lead to confusion. The story is told of a woman who was seeking God's will. She took the Bible, and let it fall open randomly. She plunged her finger at the open book and read the verse where the finger pointed. It said, "Judas went out and hanged himself." She did it again. This time her finger landed on "Go, and do thou likewise." Taking Scripture out of context can lead someone in some interesting directions.

Begin a study of the Gospels with your loved ones. Take a yellow marker and underline any verse that points to the level of commitment Jesus requires of his disciples. Underline verses about self-denial, picking up one's cross, and sacrifice. At the end of each book, discuss what you've learned about what it means to be a follower of Jesus Christ.

I recommend the timeless book *How to Read the Bible for All Its Worth*, by Gordon D. Fee and Douglas Stuart. You'll learn much about mining the richness of Scripture by reading it in context.

Finally, have a conversation with your loved ones about pastor worship. It is possible to cross the line between respect and worship! In the inner city, where corrupt preachers prey on the unsuspecting poor, it is a revolutionary act, an act of resistance, to tell people the truth about the exploitation that can take place in the church.

HOMEWORK

- Writing in your own words, sum up the meaning of the prosperity gospel. Why do you believe it has not only persisted but spread through the years?

- What stood out to you most in this chapter?

- What would you tell someone who is giving huge sums of money to a religious figure with the expectation of health, wealth, and prosperity? What would you tell a senior who is not going to take medicine any longer because the preacher said that by Jesus' stripes he or she is healed?

RETHINKING URBAN MINISTRY

*The Reverend Adam Clayton
Powell Jr.'s Road
to Social Justice Ministry*

When young Adam Clayton Powell Jr. returned home to Harlem after college in 1930, his life's work was before him. He had it made. His dad was the pastor of the most prestigious church in Harlem, and Adam had a job for life if he wanted it. His life of privilege separated him from the impoverished blacks who walked the Harlem streets beside him. He had little understanding of their plight until a doctor at Harlem Hospital approached him about a grave injustice. Even though the patient list at Harlem Hospital was completely black, the medical staff were white. The administration fired all of the black health-care providers. "What can I do?" Powell asked.[1]

The doctor said, "You have got to be what Clarence Darrow and Mayor John P. Altgeld of Chicago were to the maimed and beaten, the sightless and voiceless! The eyes and ears, and a flaming tongue crying in the wilderness for kindness and humanity and understanding."

Powell said,

> And so for the first time I heeded the call of the masses and
> became part of the struggles of the people of Harlem. . . . The
> people of the streets, the failures, the misfits, the despised,
> the maimed, the beaten, the sightless, and the voiceless had
> made a captive of me . . . and I was to know no other love
> but these people. Whenever they commanded, I followed,
> but followed only to lead.[2]

Powell not only went on to assume his father's pulpit at the
Abyssinian Baptist Church but became a US congressman and one
of the powerful preachers of his time. Malcolm X had had a
number of harsh words for ministers, but he had a genuine and
mutual respect for Powell.

Powell was a product of a ministerial culture that passed down
through generations. Pastors were called on to be community
leaders for the simple fact that they were unconnected from the
system. That is, a pastor did not have to depend on the estab-
lishment for income; the church provided the pastor's salary.
Therefore, the threat of being fired or displaced for making a stand
was not there as it would be for rank-and-file church members.
The preacher often lived next to the church building in the
parsonage and was available to the members day or night. The fact
that the pastor and the church leaders actually lived in
the community created an *us* mentality. What happened to
the members was going to directly affect the pastor by virtue
of geography.

The gains of the civil rights movement changed the mission of
many churches as well as their response to the problems of the

inner city. President Lyndon B. Johnson's legislation struck down restrictive housing covenants that had previously limited blacks, regardless of income or social stature in the same community. The black middle class left the inner cities for life in the suburbs. Pastors and church leaders often relocated to brighter horizons as well. Class barriers have existed in the black community since slave masters separated the house slaves from the field slaves. However, in post–civil rights America, that great divide was exacerbated. There is a gulf between the people who live in the 'hood and those who commute to worship there on Sundays. One of the objections of the resistance is to bridge that divide. The following story accentuates this challenge.

THE DAY THE PREACHER GOT CUSSED OUT

The most interesting thing that anyone ever emailed to me was a video filmed by a bystander of a potentially violent encounter featuring Rev. Jamal Bryant, one of America's most famous preachers, and a Baltimore 'hood activist called PFK Boom.[3] The good Rev. was clearly out of his element. He was standing in the courtyard of a Baltimore housing project. He had shed his black clerical robe and shiny black shoes for a baseball cap and leisure wear. His antagonist was one of the founding members of the 300 Gangstas. The 300 Gangstas organization was named after the film *300* about the ancient Spartan soldiers who overcame tremendous odds even though outnumbered. They were embraced by the community because they represented the forgotten, the marginalized, and the disinherited.

Boom, a reddish brown bald man with black sunglasses and the build of a welterweight boxer, approached the renowned pastor, and instead of referring to him by his honorific title he says, "Yo, can I holler at you for a second, man?" Then, "I'm the streets, man, cold-blooded, man." Communication goes downhill from there. Boom is incensed that the city's most prominent religious leader waited more than a year to visit West Wednesday, the Tyrone West vigil. And when he did show up, he came phone in hand to film the demonstration. Boom brings it to 'hood-style. He tells the pastor that he is not welcome in the streets. Bryant's response? He agrees to Boom's demand. "Alright then, I won't come on the streets," he says. Boom continues, "We don't want you in our city now. Get the [expletive] out the whole city. Is it that easy?"

As Bryant walks slowly away, wild laughter from unseen parties erupts in the background. Why were they responding to the confrontation in that manner? Boom told me later, "People looked at me like David who had just conquered Goliath."[4]

I was kind of sad when he said that. You see in previous years, the pastor would have been seen as David. Instead, people in the 'hood sometimes look at pastors as exploiters who target the poorest of the poor for photo ops, tithes, and grant money. Boom is a grassroots, feet-to-the-street community activist with unquestioned street cred. PFK stands for "Playing for Keeps," and Boom? Make of it what you will.

I wrote an article about the encounter that caught the attention of community activists in Oakland. They were profoundly moved. A phone call came, asking me, "Do you know that brother? How can we meet him?" They weren't talking about Bryant. They wanted to meet Boom. Why? Boom had stood up to the clergy, whom many see as fake and an affront to the struggle for human rights and dignity in the inner city. Soon after, Baltimore's Boom was invited to be a keynote speaker at a national conference held in Oakland on behalf of formerly incarcerated people and their allies. Boom's speech tore the house down.

One of the grave disappointments for Boom is the fact that the faith community does not commit itself to being out among the people, bringing peace, and stopping violence. There are some, he says, but the warriors for peace who wear the cloth are few and far between.

He calls me the "'hood priest." I'm not Catholic, but it's one of the greatest compliments anyone has ever paid me as a minister. But is Boom overgeneralizing? Are clergy cloistered inside church buildings and feeding off the sacrifices of the faithful, or are they imitating Jesus' model, walking the troubled streets bringing hope and light in the darkness?

AN OUTDATED MINISTRY MODEL

Boom believes when preachers are real, when they are committed to the well-being of the people in the community, they will be present in the community. I happen to agree wholeheartedly. However, many pastors will not fit into Boom's ideal. Most are not going to be fixtures in the community, conversing with people and their kids on the way to school or shaking hands with the crowd in front of the liquor store. Many will say that it is their job to raise up others to do that, but they are not interested in that sort of business, nor need they be. But where is their concept of ministry formed?

Allow me to introduce you to Rev. Charlie Sams, a composite of many ministers I've met along the way. We will meet him at the beginning of his Christian service journey, the night of his ordination.

God's new preacher. It's New Year's Eve. The church parking lot is filled to capacity. It's an unusual night. Some enter the church sanctuary because it is the arena of prayer and supplication where they welcome the new year with grace and reverence. For others, it's the good-luck stop on the way to the all-night party. But a third category of people also gathers in church tonight. New Year's Eve is the date when their dreams will collide with reality.

Charlie Sams is in that last group. He is standing in a room off-stage in an ornate, royal blue robe. He is surrounded by a group of his ministerial contemporaries. The choir is lifting up the spiritual "How I Got Over" when he gets the nod to walk through the door and over to the pulpit. As soon as the side door opens, the music rises by four decibels. The bright lights blind him momentarily. The crowd is on its feet as he leads the preachers toward the chairs behind the pulpit. Charlie Sams's brand-new robe swishes above his shiny, black Florsheim shoes as he leads the way to the appropriate seats.

Charlie Sams has waited for this moment for so long. He has watched others work the crowd into a frenzy. He has witnessed men of great oratory skill charm women with the hypnotic prowess paralleled only by the late soul singers Percy Sledge and Marvin Gaye. He has listened to dozens of poorly structured and weakly executed sermons, and now he's ready to wade into battle like a gladiator with a golden sword. His plan is to best them all. And he's good. Make no mistake about it. As soon as he takes his breath, his father leans over and whispers in his mother's ear, "Looks like we got another Bishop T. D. Jakes on our hands, baby."

At the conclusion of the service, his grandmother, who has flown to Louisiana just for this special occasion, presents Sams with a brand-new Bible. His name is engraved on the cover in gold leaf. Tears stream down Grandma's face as she hands it to him. Childhood friends pump his hands. The mothers of the church smother him with soft, red kisses. He is a licensed minister of the gospel now.

Waiting patiently. The next Sunday, Sams is invited to take his seat among the most elite members of the entire church. He is one of them now, a preacher. He sits on the pulpit stage in his designated seat, hollering amens at his pastor's sermon. After the service, church members who were not present to hear him preach on New Year's Eve grab his hand and tell him they heard that he'd been excellent. Sams's heart flutters.

After watching him cross his ankles on stage every Sunday morning for five weeks, the members begin to ask, "Charlie, when are you going to preach another sermon?"

However, that's not up to him. And it is considered the height of ill manners, bordering on blasphemy, to ask the senior pastor for the opportunity to deliver a sermon. The minister is to accept the fact that God speaks to the pastor, and when it is time for the junior pastor to preach, God will tap the senior pastor on the shoulder, and then he will in turn tap junior's shoulder.

After two months have passed, Sams begins to look around at the preachers who share the holy row with him. None of them has preached yet that year; some of them have not preached in two years. The newly minted preacher continues to holler his amens behind the pastor, but not so loudly now. For he comes to suspect that his role in this elaborate pageantry is to be little more than that of a well-dressed accessory, like a hype man for a hip-hop star.

What's gone wrong? A few things. First, Sams should understand that he should not expect to preach at this church. He will have to be pastor of his own church if he desires to use his gifts of oratory from the pulpit on a regular basis. However, he must understand that the process is quite competitive. To get started, he must find a church where the pastor has been deposed or died. He must also find a powerful clergy person or someone within the church's leadership structure who can champion his cause, a powerful ally he will forever be beholden to should his cause succeed. (If his father had been a pastor instead of a barber, his stock would have risen considerably.) Should Sams's star ever rise, he too will sit down in the seat of power wielding the scepter of authority in his fist like a child's rattle.

Until that day, Sams should not expect the pastor to relinquish any measure of his might. He once sat in Sams's seat, and when he glances behind himself mid-sermon, he recognizes the hunger in Sams's eyes because it once was his own. Now that he has risen, he guards his pride and joy, the pulpit, like an angel with a flaming sword. The pulpit, the preaching moment, is the pinnacle point of his dominance. From it, he dispenses direction, judgment, and correction. It underscores his leadership.

What would happen if the pastor gave Sams several opportunities and some faction within the church decided that they preferred Sams's preaching to his own? War could break out in the church. This is how some churches split. That would never do. As I once heard a pastor say, "You don't want to raise up another David." (Ironically, that would place him in the role of Saul.) Therefore, the pastor will broker an uneasy truce with his spiritual underlings. They will agree not to ask for too much, and he will agree not to give it to them.

Sams's big opportunity. The next decade passed uneventfully. In that time frame, Sams preached a grand total of nine sermons. Then, one day the pastor fell ill. It was pneumonia or pleurisy or something like that. On the Friday that the pastor was released from the hospital, the doctor demanded bed rest, repeating again and again that the preaching dynamo had been fortunate to arrive at the hospital on time.

Sunday was two days away. Even though the pastor was ill, services would go on. For ten years, Sams had served under the pastor without murmuring or disputing. His hair was graying now. Yet he bowed his head in obedience, as was expected. On Saturday morning, the head of the deacon board called.

"Preacher, can you be ready to preach by tomorrow?"

Minister Sams took a deep, joyous breath. At last, this was his moment. Yes, he would be ready.

The next morning Sams arrived at the church building a full two hours before the services were set to begin. He laid prostrate on the altar in the dark, humbling himself before the Lord.

At 11 a.m., the service began. The songs, prayers, and testimonies rose from the congregation.

At 11:43, the head of the deacon board took the microphone and introduced the speaker of the hour. Sams bowed his head and prayed, "Lord, speak now through thy servant."

Just as he rose to his feet, the back door swung open. A gust of wind caused the church members to shiver. They turned in their seats to take a look at the latecomer. There, in a wrinkled, white clerical robe and pink house slippers stood the pastor. He walked down the aisle pausing every few feet to throw out a cough that sounded like the call of a hungry bear. He neglected to cover his mouth. Worshipers flung their hands up to protect themselves from the showers of saliva and phlegm.

The pastor was ill-shaven. A rank odor like urine and cheap hair grease rose from him. He trembled slightly. A grumble rippled through the crowd, then a sea of soft whispers. Two of the deacons escorted him to the pulpit.

"Thank you, Sams, that'll be enough," he said.

The defeated minister stepped back and retook his seat.

"Thank you, Pastor," he said.

Without a greeting or explanation, the pastor leaned forward toward the microphone and with a death rattle in his voice, he declared, "God called me to preach, and I'm to preach."

Sams sat in his seat, head bowed. He fought back two tears that threatened to give him away. His word from the Lord would have to wait for another day.

CALLED TO PREACH VERSUS CALLED TO MINISTER

Churches are filled with associate ministers like Charlie Sams. Often they are not as gracious. Some are bitter backbiters, and others openly rebel against leaders who tell them to accept their lot as a burden from God. But if God summons a man or woman to minister and then equips him or her with the necessary gifts, could it be God's will that the person develops saddle sores from sitting on a pew each week as an exercise in tolerance? Many ministers will say God called them to preach. That's a huge difference from saying God called them to minister.

Who is a better model than Jesus of what ministry should look like? Yes, he sometimes preached (for example, the Sermon on the Mount). But more often he found himself sharing the good news at dinner parties with people of questionable character. He spent his time healing sick people; feeding the poor; chopping it up with outsiders, outcasts, and outlaws; and pouring the good news into the disciples who would one day carry on in his absence.

The book of John tells us that following that fateful, final Passover meal, Jesus poured water into a bowl. He then knelt down in the soft glow of candlelight and began to wash the red clay from between the toes of his disciples. The Savior, God Almighty, in human flesh scrubbed their nasty, stinking feet with his own garment. By the time the last disciple was seated in front of him, he might have been nauseous from the stench. His back hurt. His fingers were sore. Dirty water from the bowl splashed him in the face.

We easily remember this vivid picture, but we often forget the words at the end of this particular episode. Jesus said,

> Now that I, your Lord and Teacher, have washed your feet, you also should wash one another's feet. I have set you an example that you should do as I have done for you. Very truly I tell you, no servant is greater than his master, nor is a messenger greater than the one who sent him. Now that you know these things, you will be blessed if you do them. (John 13:14-17)

The apostle Paul informs us about Jesus,

> Who, being in very nature God,
>   did not consider equality with God something to be
>   used to his own advantage;
>   rather, he made himself nothing
>   by taking the very nature of a servant,
>   being made in human likeness. (Philippians 2:6-7)

Jesus took the role of a slave!

Jesus outlined the weapons of the resistance and redefined the essence of kingdom power. Matthew 20:25-28 says,

> Jesus called them together and said, "You know that the rulers of the Gentiles lord it over them, and their high officials exercise authority over them. Not so with you. Instead, whoever wants to become great among you must be your servant, and whoever wants to be first must be your slave—just as the Son of Man did not come to be served, but to serve, and to give his life as a ransom for many."

For Jesus, ministry wasn't defined by how much money came in through the offering. He didn't consider himself a bona fide preacher because someone followed him and carried his bag. No, that is how power is defined in the realm of darkness. Jesus equated ministry with servanthood. For Jesus, humility was the way to greatness in God's kingdom.

Humility and servanthood are compasses that will lead us in our journey to the most difficult places where ministry happens. They will teach us what to say and show us what to do. They will make us a light that will glow in the coldness of outer space. If we approach someone using the mindset Jesus describes here, we are bound to make an impact. Humility and servanthood are the minister's combat uniform.

THE WORLD NEEDS MINISTERS

The world will never have enough ministers. There will never be enough people with the humility to let God's love shine through them unhindered. You don't need any letters behind your name to wash someone's feet. You won't need the pastor's okay to mop out the bathrooms. You don't need ordination papers to go out to a homeless encampment with a big bag of sandwiches and some water bottles. No jealous preacher is likely to fight you for the opportunity to fill up your car with unchurched teenagers who need a ride to the youth group meeting. There will be no ruckus raised on the day that you decide to go down to the juvenile hall and share the word of hope with some incarcerated soul. Minister, as long as the world is broken, it will need you. It will need the tender touch of your healing hands. It will need a heart that bleeds for the broken.

The tradition that Sams was raised in has seen its day. The streets of the inner city are lined with churches just like the one he attends, and they are organized under the same rules. Those people surrounding them who need Christ will not feel compelled to enter such places. Churches like Sams's house of worship are not even designed to reach them. They might as well put a sign on the front door that says, "Broken families, people with addiction issues, the homeless, gang members, and the formerly incarcerated *not welcome*." Mark my words, one day many of those gothic buildings will be converted into condominiums and skating rinks.

The sad thing is that Sams might well choose to go down with the ship. Unless something drastically changes, Sams will never be afforded the opportunity to use his God-given gifts, which is a shame. Many lives could be changed by his ministry if he redefined ministry as serving rather than preaching. At some point, the beleaguered Sams will have to ask himself, *Did God call me to sit here and observe ministry or did he call me to do it?* The resistance needs sleeping giants like Sams to wake up. The impact of a legion of these ministers committed to the struggle for spiritual renewal, soul salvation, and social justice in the 'hoods of America would change everything!

One of the most powerful phrases in the preacher's handbook is "God called me." Think for a moment about what that should mean to you. Almighty God—the shaper of the worlds, Lord of the universe, the keeper of Judgment Day, the one who hung the stars in the expanse of outer space, the architect of the amoeba, and the physicist who designed our sun—whispered into your ear and said, "I have something I want you to do. I am calling you!" Did God call you to sit behind the senior pastor playing idiot savant, clapping every time he makes a dramatic pause, or did God have a greater plan for your gifts? Will you let your gifts rot on the front row, or will you use them to build the resistance? What would it mean for you personally to take your gifts outside of the church building?

HOMEWORK

- Write an essay answering these questions: What is the difference between a minister and a preacher? Was Rev. Sams fulfilled in his calling? What went wrong for Sams? What might he have done differently? Why didn't the pastor invest more in Sams and the others ministers in the church? Are there ways in which you have become Sams?

- What will you do next?

11 WAGING PEACE

To Be Called God's Child

In the Sermon on the Mount, Jesus said, "Blessed are the peacemakers, for they will be called the children of God" (Matthew 5:9). Members of the resistance must take that seriously. No longer can we watch the morning news to find out there was another homicide in our city, yawn, and say, "What, Ma? Pancakes for breakfast again?" Jesus Christ calls us to be violence interrupters and reconcilers.

When I was a kid, to be a peacemaker was to negotiate an end to a fistfight between two equals. Today, it is so much more complicated to stop a beef from escalating into bloodshed in the 'hood. Peacemaking is a complicated process. In the inner city, unseen issues are often at the root of the rage that makes one person want to shoot another. The fact that your kids are hungry, that you can't find a job, that rats scurry across your living room floor at night, that you are living with red-hot trauma years after you've experienced or witnessed hellish violence can serve as the trigger that causes you to blank out and commit some unspeakable crime.

Do you want to be a peacemaker? If you are responsible for bringing resources into an impoverished community, you are creating peace in the community. If you are teaching someone job skills or helping someone create a résumé, you are indirectly creating peace. If you are warring against the prison industrial complex, you are a peacemaker.

Have I ever jumped into the middle of a violent situation involving two strangers to stop them from getting seriously hurt? Yes. However, in the 'hood we don't necessarily have to create peace that way. We can create peace by sending money to a proven after-school program. We can create peace by helping someone learn English as a second language or hosting a recovery group. We can be peacemakers by sending funds to someone equipped to intercede in negative situations. Peace is complicated in the twenty-first century. But the good news is there are many ways to wage it. I will introduce you to someone who does it as his "get down" (his calling or vocation).

BLESSED ARE THE PEACEMAKERS

When the godfather of gangsta rap, Ice-T, walks into a booth and creates a theme song for your life, your street cred is unquestioned. When the man who penned songs like "New Jack Hustler," "OG," and "6 in the Morning" is so impressed with your life that he asks to produce a television show about your everyday comings and goings, you are not from the streets, you *are* the streets. That is true of Malik Spellman, an LA gang intervention specialist. After the second season of *The Peacemaker: L.A. Gang Wars* was finished, I downloaded all of the episodes. True, some of the parts are staged. However, the stories are real. So much so that the epilogue of each episode tells us who lived and who didn't after the cameras stopped rolling.

Spellman's mission is simple. He diffuses conflicts between rival gangs. It's dangerous work done with little financial remuneration. In fact, the people Spellman serves are leery of nonprofit hustlers and exploitative preachers. His success is rooted in part by the fact that he doesn't make money off of his peacemaking efforts. There have been times when someone's life depended on Spellman's ability to race from location A to location B when his gas tank was on *E*. Grace allowed him to make the trip without running out of fuel. Sometimes street figures who revere his work will put a few dollars in his pocket for gas. For Spellman, the level of community respect needed to do what he does is more important than money.

The first thing that strikes me about Spellman is his passion for those in distress. He tells stories of how he has driven from one 'hood to the other struggling to intervene before warring gangs started shooting. His life vibrates with purpose. He once had a dream in which God was calling his soul home. In the dream, Spellman responded, "God, I can't die today. I got something to do."

Usually, when I make an appointment to interview someone by phone, they are settled in a quiet place alone. Not Spellman. When I called Spellman, he had a young woman—he didn't introduce her by name—on the other line of a three-way call. But Spellman did say that she was incarcerated in a state prison facility. His exact words were, "She's Harriet Tubman on the underground railroad. We have to be swift with her thing. It's a movement. If the phone gets off, it is because she is incarcerated. She's eighteen years locked down." No, Spellman wouldn't get off the phone for a book interview when lives were hanging in the balance. He would have to multitask.[1]

What was Spellman's business with the sister on the line? She was assisting him in negotiating a gang truce in the streets of LA. If you're like me, you wonder, how can someone in a maximum security prison, spiritually as far away from the streets as the earth is from the moon, negotiate a peace treaty in a war-torn 'hood? Spellman explained, "[We create peace] by talking to sisters like this and getting them to talk to people in the dayroom, and the people in the dayroom will come back to them, and they put a report out on the streets, giving us a license to operate. There's never been a female truce for gangs, and that's what we working on right now."

I posed my next question to the sister he referred to as "Harriet Tubman." She was about twenty years old when she was locked up, the mother of one child. Now she is thirty-eight and still looking at a lengthy sentence through a dark tunnel.

She began to talk about how the war on drugs was throwing scores of black women down the well of incarceration. She also spoke about the crisis of excessive sentencing. "As soon as they get eighteen, they're sent here," she said.

How does one wind up in the concrete slave ship? I asked. Harriet Tubman answered, "Not enough resources. Everybody is basically in the same struggle. So basically, we don't have any guidance to know what to do to get out of the situation that we're in. When you are in a gang, that is not your focus. Priorities are different. Our beliefs are different. So we're not thinking about how we can get out of the situation. We are basically in the situation."

In Oakland there's a saying: gang life will eventually lead you to one of two destinations—prison or death. I assume that it's the same for LA. Knowing this, why would anyone join a gang? Harriet Tubman said,

That's all they know, and that's what they assume. If my parents are in it, that's what I'm going to do.

Subconsciously parents encourage their children to be involved because they have them in that environment. And they keep them around those type of people. They don't know that the kids are absorbing everything that is going on around them, and they think that is the thing to do. Kids assume that this is all right to do because this is my parents, and their friends are all in it.

Spellman said,

Kids are born in a time of war. When you see kids gravitate toward gangs, what else can you do when you have a community that is disenfranchised, marginalized through crack cocaine and HIV, when you have chemicals and biological weapons of mass destruction, drink, drugs, pills, and guns readily available? What else are you going to do when you got no love in the household? Kids are going to gravitate to where they are comfortable.

Spellman has written a book titled *Mama, Why Did You Choose This Block?* It's a question that a kid in a notorious gang neighborhood might ask his mother as he is pressured to join by peers. Speaking of gang members, Spellman said, "They are social beings like the rest, so they gravitate to those who have something in common with them, a broken household."

MAKING PEACE

"What can the church do, Malik?" I asked.

From here Spellman's voice crackled with anger. He expressed dismay that the church has benefited handsomely over decades from the multitude of homicide funerals that it charges poor people to perform. He is disturbed that the church is the most well-funded institution in the black community and yet no one seems to know where all of the money goes. Spellman has ideas where it should go. He said, *out.*

Take some of that money and put it into a legal fund. Help some of those people from your communities who are behind bars to mount cases.

Each one of these churches has lawyers in their congregations. Confront the issue of all of these mothers behind bars! This sister [referring to "Harriet Tubman"] helped me with a million gang truces from behind the walls. She's been working with me for the past fifteen years stopping gang violence. So where is the social equity at? That's what I need to know. Release her to the streets and let her wage the peace in the streets of war.

Spellman wasn't done. Outrage and disappointment shook his voice as he spoke about what he perceived as the church's negligence in helping the disinherited in communities decimated by gang warfare. Occasionally, he used hardcore profanity to accentuate his points.

And *you*, pastor! And *you*, church! If the Rev. Dr. Martin Luther King Jr. whom you revere was here today, he'd be on his knees on the concrete cleaning up the blood!

And *you* pastor! Step up or step back.

And *you*, church, get out of that church building and into these streets. Put your feet down on the concrete and wipe the blood with your hands.

Spellman's rage grew tangible. It was like I was on the witness stand in the court of God. "And *you*, pastor! And *you*, church!" he thundered over and over again.

And *you*, church, I'm begging the church from coast to coast, help us get our sisters free!

And *you*, pastor, Lazarus is laid out in front of your church door. While he is pissing and [defecating] in front of your Christian church, you are saying that you represent Jesus Christ? What are you going to do for Lazarus, *pastor*? Cause there is a severe penalty for fake pastors, a severe swift penalty. Some of you are just ambulance whores chasing the next headline. So right now it's all fun and games because God is working on God's time. He's in no rush. For any human being who thinks this is a game, the next stop is God. Your congregation and your Rolls Royce will not be able to help you in hell.

To these rich preachers, do you know there is a God? Some of you preachers are just professional organizers and extrapolators. How dare you! You play and gamble with your anointing! Stop leading these black people into quadruple darkness and thinking God is not taking account. To the guilty pastors, you have transgressed all boundaries. God is swift to take account.

Spellman talked so heavily about the fires of hell that await pastors who neglect the poor that my scalp started sweating. As he spoke, I was searching my own life and earnestly praying about my own faithfulness to God's mission.

WHAT DO YOU SEE IN MY FACE?

"Go to 6th and Julius if you want to see the future for our people," Spellman said, referring to the skid row section of Los Angeles. "It's a modern-day plantation or holocaust camp. You'll see a barrel there with rats eating out of the side. Dogs are pissing on the side, and we got our people drinking water out of it, and we cool with it. We are unmoved. It doesn't bother us."

One day, while walking into a store in that area, a homeless woman walked by Spellman. Instead of mascara, she had used roofing tar for mascara and eyebrow liner. She turned to him and asked, "How do I look?"

Spellman responded, "You look beautiful, sister. Just beautiful."

Before I hung up the phone that night, I asked, "Malik, are you ever afraid?"

He said, "No. Because when I'm out in the street and I look into the eyes of the people, in those eyes I see myself, and I'm never afraid of myself."

Why is the peacemaker able to put his life on the line time and again? It goes back to what he sees when he looks into the eyes of the people he ministers to. He sees beauty and reflections of his own humanity.

Imagine, if church members actually saw Jesus in the faces of the poor who surround their church buildings? Would they leave him out in the streets unattended, or would they wash his wounds? The line between those two possible answers is the bridge between the old wineskins and the resistance.

HOMEWORK

- Watch an episode of the TV show *The Peacemaker: L.A. Gang Wars*. (You can find it on YouTube or iTunes.) Write a paper about it. What elements of this book come to mind as you watch the show?

12 STORIES FROM THE STREETS

Where Do We Belong?

When someone is waist deep in the criminal underworld, we say they are "'bout that life." If you were to ask someone who is 'bout that life where their activities take place, they would point to a street corner or a 'hood. Like a salesperson, they want to put themselves in a situation where they can peddle their wares to as many people as possible. Even though it is illegal, the dope game cannot exist without some level of visibility. When you think about it, if we are committed to the kingdom of God, we are fighting for the same pool of clientele that is being served by the drug dealers. The exception is that most Christian ministry takes place within the comfort and four walls of an air-conditioned church building. Often, we apathetically concede the streets to the devil.

People believe that if the enemy shows up in a church service, they'll see a scene straight out of *The Exorcist*. No, Satan's much more subtle than that. His trademarks are lethargy, laziness, and apathy. He understands the power we possess in Christ. He also knows that he will have a big problem on his hands if we figure that out and start to use it. So he wants us to be consumed with leisure, pleasure, and comfort. He knows that if we ever hit our knees praying "Oh, God, use me for your kingdom," he'd be in trouble. And if the church as a collective began to burn with that desire, it's over. So that's why he keeps us consumed with the fish fry, the annual church picnic, or the building-fund drive. He tells us that it's too dangerous to go outside with the gospel. He wants us inside where it's safe—for him.

If the drug dealers operated as we do, they'd go broke. Instead, they put themselves among the lost. They often don't even speak. They just maintain a presence, and when someone wants what they have to offer, the distance is short. There are many churches that operate with the exact same mindset. I have pastor friends who have one foot on the block, often because they came from the block and understand that world. They represent the resistance.

I want to introduce you to a few people I have met along the way whose names ring out on the block. Follow me to Chicago.

WALKING THE STREETS OF CHICAGO'S SOUTH SIDE

A summer haze wafts through the air as I step out of the taxi and onto the hot asphalt streets of Chicago's South Side. I had never been to Chicago before, but I wasn't there sightseeing. I turn my sights toward the front of St. Sabina's Catholic Church. A certain sadness sinks down over me even now as I think back on it. In front of the great stone structure is a glass enclosure that contains the school pictures of perhaps one hundred children. Those smiling faces don't belong to kids who just won the spelling bee or made the honor roll. All of those children lost their lives to violence in this neighborhood, perhaps the vast majority of them to gunfire. A flashing sign high above the street pleads: "Our Children Deserve the Chance to Grow Up."

I was there because I saw an announcement on Facebook about a march through this 'hood, a march for peace. The march was scheduled to coincide with the last day of school. Summer in the 'hood brings an explosion of violence and lost lives: the massive unemployment, boredom, and frustration are the devil's stew.

St. Sabina's is led by one of the most widely respected inner-city clergy persons in the United States. His 'hood pass is platinum. Rev. Dr. Michael Pfleger is an enigma of sorts, a white pastor who leads one of the most socially conscious, activist churches in America; he helps with the struggle for black life in a place where its value is dropping daily. He is a Catholic priest who preaches like a Pentecostal revivalist. He has been embraced by black leaders from the late Maya Angelou to the late Mrs. Coretta Scott King, from Bishop T. D. Jakes to Minister Louis Farrakhan. Even his detractors can't deny his fearlessness. He has confronted evil forces who threaten the way of life in his community, whether they be gang lords or government officials. Recently, he received international attention by publicly calling out the gang-affiliated gangsta rapper Chief Keef, ordering him to "shut up!"

When I first saw Father Pfleger walking down the street that hot afternoon wearing a black shirt and clergy collar, he was standing in front of some school-age children. He didn't know me from Adam, so I got close enough to hear the conversation. He knew those children by name. He asked questions about their grades, about their summer plans, about their dreams. He loved them, and they loved him. In a world where so much is not as it should be for children, this was a beautiful scene.

As the sun began to slip low in the Midwestern sky, a crowd followed the preacher to the front of the church building. Many people there had huge portraits of lost young black men slaughtered in these streets. People all around me were shedding tears. As Father Pfleger climbed the granite stairs, a cadre of bodyguards began to surround him. A bank of TV cameras and microphones cut off his forward progress. Neighborhood folks, almost all of them black, squeezed through the phalanx, grabbing for a handshake. He was a symbol of hope climbing the granite steps, the visible image of one person who refused to be stopped in his crusade to stop the bloodshed. It was warm outside, but I felt chills.

A youth choir sang gospel songs that rose high above the bloody streets and toward the clouds that floated above the mayhem. The chief of the Chicago Police Department spoke about a particularly brutal shooting that had taken place at a children's picnic in the 'hood earlier that day. Then it was Father Pfleger's time. A ball of fire, he decried the crisis of bullets flying through the streets. He implored the people to make a stand. You could feel faith and resolve move the crowd. The preacher told the people they would have to fight for the future. People were shouting, "Amen!"

When he was finished it was dark. Then he said something like, "It's time. Let's go."

SOME BELIEVERS JUMP INTO
THE STRUGGLE AND SOME DON'T

The crowd that night had swollen ten times from the beginning of the rally to the end when the march was to take place. Soon a thousand chanting marchers looked like one long black snake moving through the streets of the South Side. I talked to a number of people that night, including a mother who had lost her son to gunfire. I asked, "Ma'am, I saw a number of community leaders who were recognized for standing with St. Sabina's tonight, but I didn't hear anything said about the local pastors. Aren't the other preachers from this neighborhood standing with this campaign against violence?"

She said:

In order to have empathy for the people who are living here, you have to be here. You have to really know them. You have to be a part of their lives. That's where you get the thirst to stand for them. Most of the pastors and church members of these other churches don't actually live here. They come in to do services on Sunday and Wednesday, and then they go back to the suburbs. They don't even know us.

When my opportunity came to speak to Father Pfleger (or Father Mike, as he prefers to be called), he said that in the early days of his ministry, he invited other local churches time and again. He was often rebuffed for various reasons. However, Operation Push, headed by the Rev. Jesse Jackson, and the Nation of Islam did pledge support. After a while, Father Mike gave up on many of the churches near his diocese. He said, "I wasn't giving that any more energy. They have seemed to close their eyes to it. It's shameful."[1]

Father Mike believes that if churches across America made a concerted effort to be a presence in their inner-city communities, that step alone would cause a drop in violent crime. He is perplexed why most congregations do not step out of the doors of their buildings to be a witness to the community.

He said:

The majority of Jesus' ministry was all outside. In the early church, much of the ministry was outside the walls. Today, the church has become another Fortune 500 company. What makes the church authentic is not what we do inside the building; ministry happens largely outside. In the story of the Mount of Transfiguration, the disciples saw the glory of God and wanted to build tents on the mountain. However, it wasn't God's will for them to remain on the mountaintop. When they came down the mountain, they were surrounded by the people. That's where the ministry took place.

When you fall in love with Jesus, it causes you to fall in love with the community. If you read and study Jesus, he spent his life with the blind and the lame, the throwaway people. If we say we are following Jesus, that's where we will find ourselves, among them.

You've got to reach out to the gang members. Love them. Respect them. Offer them options and alternatives. You can't just say put down the gun and have nothing for them to pick up. Create job-training programs. Stabilize them. Don't just demonize them.

IDENTITY THEFT

Pastor Mike told me that the church is suffering from what he calls "identity theft." Believers have been commissioned to move beyond the walls of the church to touch the hurting and walk alongside the lost. Christians are to be the voice against those who would prey on the poor. However, for the priest from Chicago, the body of Christ is not living up to that call.

Father Pfleger said:

> The greatest institution that I believe has failed America is the church. . . . We claim to walk in and be the voice of Christ in the world; be the voice for the poor, the disenfranchised, and I really believe that church has become another Fortune 500 company. . . . We forget that our voice is to be a voice of conscience. We need to be asking the questions no one else asks. . . . We need to be sitting at a table where we're not invited and demanding that at those tables we speak for the poor and the forgotten.[2]

Father Pfleger also said:

> Who would not agree that liquor stores are pimping us? They sell alcohol in our neighborhoods and then they take the resources from something that destroys people out of the community at night. The church, on the other hand, pays no taxes that would go to build up the community. Therefore the church should pay the community in service to it. If that's not why we exist, to be a servant for the people, we are pimping the people just like the liquor store.
>
> A lot of pastors want to build megachurches. I'd rather have a church that is like Ebenezer Baptist Church in Atlanta, Georgia [Martin Luther King Jr.'s home church]. It has a megaimpact.[3]

THE REALITY OF DANGER

I couldn't end a conversation with one of America's foremost inner-city ministers without mentioning the elephant in the room: fear. If urban ministry were easy, we wouldn't need a resistance movement to turn up the flames of passion for the lost and the broken. Here, we are talking about doing ministry in a place where bullets fly and drugs are sold hand-to-hand. Church leaders have told me that they will not go into the mission field right in front of their churches quite simply because they are afraid. There are many pastors who do not lead their congregations into the streets near their churches because they personally are afraid. I asked Father Mike if he had any advice for clergy facing that dilemma.

"If they are afraid, they should get out of the pulpit!"

Later he muses, "The church in my mind should be dangerous to evil. Evil should run when the church is the church."

When he was a teenager, Father Mike saw Martin Luther King Jr. attacked in a park in Father Mike's Chicago neighborhood. Seeing the price tag that came with social justice strengthened his resolve. He also keeps pictures of freedom fighters he admires on the wall in his church office. They remind him to be strong in the face of adversity.

The path hasn't been easy. Under Father Mike's leadership, St. Sabina's Church has built housing for the homeless and the elderly, successfully brought down the crime rate in the community, created peace between warring street entities, helped scores of people land jobs, sent many young people to college, and done dozens of other things that have given a chance to the disinherited.

Along the way, Father Mike has had an adopted son shot to death as a result of getting caught in the crossfire of two rival gangs. Father Mike has been spit on, beat up, and threatened. He's had a Fox News commentator refer to him as everything but Satan because of his insistence that systemic racism exists in America.

I asked Father Mike how he got to know so many people in the community on a personal basis. His answer was straightforward. He lives in the community where he ministers, and he is a consistent presence in the streets. We laughed as we discussed *On the Waterfront*, a movie we both loved about a priest whose theology forces him to broaden his understanding of his church to encompass the entire community.

Father Mike said,

People often ask me about the size of my congregation. I have many, many members. You see, the people who actually come to my church only constitute a small portion of my members. The whole neighborhood is actually my congregation: the ones who come in and join and actually the people who stand shoulder to shoulder with me as soldiers as we go out to minister in the community. If you are in this neighborhood, whether you have ever walked through the doors of my church or not, I see you as a member of my congregation.

Father Mike has redefined the parameters of the church. His members are not simply the tithers or even the attendees. They are the people in his community, people who need the church's help but may never actually join its rolls. The resistance calls us to broaden our spheres of love and service. So do the times.

ON THE STREETS

Earlier in this book, I mentioned the cyclone of economic devastation that gentrification and homelessness have wrought in Oakland. Hungry people drift up and down International, a black asphalt tract of land that runs from one end of East Oakland to the other. Tent cities line the streets of the 'hood. This is an America I never thought I would see; nevertheless, it's here. This battlefield is not without its warriors. One of them is Rev. Joseph Jones, pastor of Alpha and Omega Foundation and Worship Center. Behind a corrugated steel fence painted with purple crosses sits a tent with folding chairs on a dirt floor. From a wooden pulpit in front of the space, Rev. Jones preaches his nightly sermons when weather permits. When it doesn't, he is known to drive the streets in the predawn hours, inviting the homeless into the warmth of his church sanctuary for hot chocolate and pastries. On the streets it's easy to find out who is real and who isn't because the people trapped here will tell you with no hesitation, and they love the tall preacher with a flat-top haircut and glasses who laughs easily and is always quick with a Scripture or a joke.

Rev. Jones knows more about homelessness in post-civil rights America than many sociologists. In an interview he said,

> Homeless people are trapped in a tar pit. They are stuck in a rat trap and they can't get out. They are caught in something a person can't get free of by themselves. If someone is homeless, they need someone to throw them a lifeline. Someone has to help. You hear about celebrities who were once homeless. You never hear them say that they got out by themselves. There was someone who took the time to help them.
>
> Homeless people are all connected to somebody. Everybody has a biological family. Everyone has friends whether they are still in contact or not. It's not that these people were born homeless. They are just disconnected. They went to school somewhere. Some of them went to college. Every face that you see has a story, some more than one.[4]

Jones reveals how he connects with the disconnected and how he empowers them to help themselves. The episode calls to mind the story in Luke 5:17-26, where some dear friends brought their paralyzed buddy to Jesus on a mat. Jones says,

> There was a man living here in Oakland who was paralyzed. He was homeless. He lived underneath the 580 freeway. He had rats crawling on top of his body. He couldn't get up. Something went down, and all of his friends who had been helping him went to jail. They were in jail for thirty days. When they got out, the first thing they did was run to make sure that he was still alive. They called the paramedics. The fire department came. They pulled him out from underneath the freeway. They sent him to the hospital. After that, he wound up in a rehabilitation center. The rehabilitation center called us when his time there was up, saying that he had nowhere to go. We took the guy in. We got him in, reconnected him with his finances. We got him reconnected with his mental health professionals, and we helped him to get reconnected spiritually. It put him in a different frame of mind. We reconnected him with his family. He got his own place and now he's doing well. He just needed to be reconnected.

Jones believes that homelessness in Oakland is worse than it has ever been. He said,

> There are kids now seventeen, eighteen, and nineteen years old that are out here hungry and homeless. I get phone calls from kids as young as fifteen and sixteen years old seeking residential housing. I have to tell them, you're not old enough

to come here. They weren't always in that situation. It is not aliens in a spaceship that dropped them off. These are members of society that got disconnected. We have to find ways to reconnect them.

BURNING-BUSH MINISTRY

The cry of the people and the call of God summoned Larry Austin, an Oakland pastor, from the safety of a loving church and a steady paycheck onto the streets of some of the city's most dangerous neighborhoods. He has a message for the 'hood: Jesus cares.

Minister Larry travels with a small sound system and a microphone. When the moment is right, he stops his car and sets up. He says,

> I call it my burning-bush ministry. The bush was there to get Moses' attention. [God] had to get Moses closer to get him to pay attention. People hear the music whether it's in a park or in front of a liquor store, and they draw closer. It has become a thrill to me. I feel empty when I'm not doing it. I've seen the people get refreshed. Jesus saw that the people were harassed and helpless. This is what compelled Jesus to go. When he gave me his eyes, I was able to see the people as he saw them. I am compelled to go to them.[5]

"Evangelism beyond the walls keeps the church from becoming some elitist social club who have forgotten the mud that they were pulled out of," said Pastor Larry. The hip-hop preacher believes that it is sinful to worship God inside a building and then walk past people who are suffering on the outside when we emerge from God's presence.

Not long ago, Pastor Larry and his church members held a Sunday morning service at a homeless encampment in Oakland. They came prepared to preach, sing, and pray. They also brought delicious, hot, soul-food dinner to serve. Pastor Larry said, "I was walking back from that exchange when I heard one guy tell another guy, 'Go on and get you one of them plates.' He said this, 'Make sure you get some of those greens. It got meat in it.'"

As Pastor Larry prepared to leave the encampment he said,

My mind went to the person who was cooking those green beans. They weren't there that day. When they were cooking those greens, they weren't cooking them like, *Let me just throw these together and give them to these people.* No, they were cooking those green beans like they were making them for their family. *I'm not going to skimp with this, because I'm going to be eating it.* The person was cooking for brothers and sisters they didn't know but they were cooking it looking at Jesus.

Later Pastor mused that a church that seeks to constantly receive from God's hand but does not give to others is a sick and spiritually deformed institution. He believes that a program of giving and service causes life to erupt and flow in a church.

YOU DON'T HAVE TO GO FAR

Regina's Door, a vintage clothing shop in downtown Oakland, is sandwiched between a number of eclectic eateries and boutiques. One thing separates Regina's Door from the other businesses on that street. It is a healing place for people who have been trafficked, abused, or violated. It is also a haven for young artists and homeless youth.

A few years ago, a young lady came to me and said, "I have been put out on the street and I have nowhere to go." Regina Evans, owner of the store said, "Give her my phone number." When I spoke to the at-risk youth again, she told me that Regina had given her a place to stay. A Regina's Door benefactor took the teenager on a shopping spree. At that time, Regina's Door was the bridge between that teenager and disaster. Regina was there for a total stranger.

In a recent conversation, Regina and I discussed the horror of human trafficking, which has stolen the lives of so many people in Oakland. Many of the trafficking victims are children. Regina is one of the leading abolitionists in the city, fighting the scourge of modern-day, inner-city slavery and giving aid to its victims.[6]

Such a terrible thing might seem overwhelming. It is. Mama Reg (as she is called in the community) did not have the money to create a safe house. She did not have the wherewithal to help children on the run to escape. However, Regina found a way to help people who had been bruised and torn apart by trauma. She created a space where they could write poetry, host discussion groups, dance, and embrace. Last winter, she was invited to visit the United Nations headquarters for a conference on 61st Commission on the Status of Women. She took fifteen young people with her. Some of them had never been out of Oakland. Love and sheer will have been her teammates in her life-saving mission.

Mama Reg said,

The strongest force is love. We think that love is easy, soft, and mushy. It's not easy. You will be stretched when you decide to delve into true love. It's bruising. We have to have patience and resilience. Love is hard but necessary if we are going to save our kids. Walking through the process with young people can be beautiful, but it can hurt. You have to be in relationship with people in order to love them. If love is the greatest force there is, you'll want to be in community with people on a daily basis. If you want to make a difference, be willing to have your life disrupted and be uncomfortable for the sake of another person.

YOU ARE THE LEADER

In order for the church to break through and become the force that transforms a flicker into a raging fire, we need a resistance. We need people with the courage and passion to leave their safety and comfort and walk into the streets with blazing hearts in search of souls that need healing. Don't wait for someone to give you permission. When Jesus gave the Great Commission, he gave us permission. Not everyone will walk to a street corner with a bullhorn. Use the unique gifts God has given you to step up to the task. Just as the times are different today, don't be afraid to be different in your approach.

Many inner-city churches have functioned as they presently are since the Great Migration of the 1940s, but that no longer works today. This is because some people benefit from things remaining just as they are. If true change comes, they will no longer be calling the shots. That's why they fear change. Some leaders would rather see the church dwindle spiritually and numerically than to let someone else lead.

Don't be bound by the past. Think outside of the box. If God gives you an idea that can bring hope and elevate people in dark places, go with it. Some people won't sign on because it isn't their idea or they can't lead it. Go for it anyway.

The church is going to look and feel different in the future. More churches will meet in coffee shops than in cathedrals. Don't be surprised if you see a dramatic rise in the number of bivocational pastors. Some of the greatest social-justice preachers might now be learning their ABCs.

Don't be afraid to be John the Baptist in the wilderness. Don't worry if your styles don't fit expectations. Let radical love be your guiding light. Put yourself on the Jericho Roads of this world. For we are the resistance. And in the words made famous in the civil rights movement, "We shall overcome."

HOMEWORK

- What do the community servants you have read about in this chapter have in common? Do most focus on journeying with the forgotten, the lost, and the broken? Why or why not?

- Write a letter to a church that has become complacent and challenge the members to take the message and the mercy of the risen Christ outside of the building.

13 PROXIMITY

The Last Lesson

From the words "follow me" to the empty tomb, what an amazing adventure it had been—full of twists and turns, the astounding and the heartbreaking—and now it culminated on the edge of the Mount of Olives, just outside Jerusalem. Here an eternity of questions and answers is crammed into one final command:

> All authority in heaven and on earth has been given to me. Therefore go and make disciples of all nations, baptizing them in the name of the Father and of the Son and of the Holy Spirit, and teaching them to obey everything I have commanded you. And surely I am with you always, to the very end of the age. (Matthew 28:18-20)

The resistance exploded with the utterance of one single word: *go*. There's no room for apathy or complacency. *Go* is a verb. It leads the hearers to cross seas, climb mountains, sleep in dungeons, and face whips and crosses. Along the way it brought eternal life to people who never would have heard of Jesus Christ if the earliest believers complacently turned Jesus' lessons into course material for a symposium.

Go. We are colaborers with Jesus. That's an exciting proposition. We are in this journey to take this Jesus to a love-starved world that needs to not only hear his quoted words but see his imitated actions. In Acts 10:38, Peter said Jesus "went around doing good." Jesus didn't go into the 'hood hollering "turn or burn!" He healed, he visited the lonely, he danced at weddings, he taught, and he journeyed with folks. He went around doing good. Often that would lead to a dialogue about faith; sometimes it didn't. However, even when he didn't verbalize it, he lived it. Every interaction God leads you to will not end in a profession of faith. However, in going as an agent of God's resistance, be faithful and be present.

Presence is essential. Read through the Gospels. Notice how many interactions and miracles happen because Jesus simply crosses paths with someone at the right time. He is walking where the people are, and then the miracles happen. Let's take this one step further. Jesus' message was rooted in illustrations that people readily understood because he journeyed closely with the people he wanted to reach. Because he lived in close proximity with them, he knew how they thought, what made them laugh, and what stories captivated them.

If you are a pastor or a Sunday school teacher, you need proximity to the people you want to reach. How else will you know what concerns them? How else will you be able to speak their language? Jesus used stories about fish and fig trees because the people readily related to these things. Do you know enough about the people in the world you minister to craft sermons they can relate to?

I learn more about Oakland by riding the buses and walking its streets than I ever could from a newspaper. I didn't have to look up a website to understand that my city is grappling with homelessness. I don't drive. So, I ride next to California's poorest people every time I go somewhere. I hear the concerns of everyday folks as they hold conversations in the soul-food restaurant. I don't have to tell you what *I* think. I can tell you what *they* think because for years I've listened to their voices. To be effective in ministry, it's necessary to hear what's on their hearts.

FRIED CHICKEN IN A DRUG BAZAAR

I work not far from an open-air drug bazaar. On my way home one night, I prayed, "God, speak to me," as I approached a block where hundreds of people milled around, going everywhere and nowhere at once, and drugs were covertly moving hand-to-hand. Minutes later, I spoke to a woman in a wheelchair on the side of the parade of humanity. I nodded and said hi. When I got a few feet away, she called to me, "Hey, hey! Can you help me?"

I walked back in her direction, and we talked. Her face was wrinkled alabaster. She couldn't have weighed more than seventy pounds. Her teeth were gone.

"How can I help you?" I asked.

"I dropped my book. Can you pick it up for me?"

Well, she had dropped a number of things: a well-worn paperback, a pink woolen scarf, a green Bic lighter, and a glass pipe, burned black from use.

I picked up the book and the scarf but left the lighter and the crack pipe where they were. Our conversation turned to God and how deeply God loved her. She told me her name. She said she used to go to church and asked if I knew the name of her pastor, which I didn't. I told her where she could find my Bible study right there in that neighborhood. And then a thought hit me. I had purchased some fried chicken at the supermarket. The delicious pieces sat in a plastic dome in the bag that dangled from my right hand.

"Are you hungry?" I asked her.

"Yes."

"Do you like fried chicken?"

"Do I!"

I reached into the bag and retrieved the plastic dome full of fried chicken. Her face took on an angelic glow as she reached out for the food. She held the plastic dome to her face in a loving embrace before she dropped it into her lap. Then she blessed me as I walked away.

As I fought the cold winds blowing in from the Pacific that night, I wondered why so many believers can quote the Great Commission and yet so few come down to a block like this to share the good news and the love of Christ.

OUT AND AMONG THE PEOPLE

One afternoon a few weeks ago I ran into a very committed community worker. She is someone I respect a great deal. I asked her some of the questions that I continue to wrestle with concerning the church and the 'hood. "Tell me something, sister," I said. "Why aren't more pastors leading the struggle to save lives in the 'hood? Why isn't the church's major thrust rescuing lives from drugs, gang life, and poverty?" She dropped this on me:

> You have to be out in this world, out in these streets among the people on a consistent basis to develop the sort of empathy and compassion for people that stretch you to do all you can to make a difference. It's not enough to understand

at a head level; you have to understand at a heart level. That comes from touching the people, walking with them in their world, on their physical plane, in their pain, sharing in their laughter, being present in the streets where they are present. Without that, you might be a well-meaning person, but you're not going to be a crusader willing to lead a mission to empower people who desperately need help.

Bronx Tale is a film about a young boy who falls beneath the spell of Sonny, a gangster who controls the neighborhood where the boy lives with his family. The movie takes place in the late fifties and early sixties. One day Sonny explains his life choices to his protégé:

> I could live anywhere I want to. You know why I live in this neighborhood? Availability. I stay close to everything. Because being on the spot, I can see trouble immediately. Trouble is like a cancer. You gotta get it early. . . . That's what it comes down to, availability. The people in this neighborhood who are on my side, they feel safe because they know I'm close and that gives them more reason to love me, but the people who want to do otherwise, they think twice because they know I'm close.[1]

Pastor, to represent the resistance is to be present. It is to see your entire community as the church's parish, not simply a handful of families on the church rolls. It is to love your parish and embrace its people. You are the shepherd of *all* the people who live in the 'hood where your church exists. When you do this, community members will look at you like Sonny in the *Bronx Tale* because you're close.

GOD SAID . . .

One person can't touch all wounds of the city. One church cannot heal all the hurt. We need a movement that will shake off the apathy and solider on with compassion. That, my friend, would be the resistance.

If you've grown up in a Bible-based community, the most profound spiritual concepts can fade in meaning like a red linen shirt that has been washed too many times. Perhaps the most powerful word given from God has lost its profundity in many hearts simply because we use it so often and so broadly that we rarely give thought to what it means and costs. The word I speak of is *love*. We say, "I love everybody." "I love the whole world." Do you? Can you? And if you do, what does that mean? What does that look like in clear, literal terms?

When a teacher of the law tries to trap Jesus in a theological argument in Luke 10, Jesus moves from the nebulous to the concrete. He begins to talk about love. He begins by quoting the well-known Torah command to love God with one's all and then gives the second command, "Love your neighbor as yourself." In verse 29, the teacher of the law asks, "And who is my neighbor?" The word *love* can be nebulous, but Jesus gives it flesh and life by connecting the word *love* to a living, breathing human being, a mugging victim on the Jericho Road. Now it's more than a philosophical concept; it's a concrete reality.

Too often, we let the people we minister to become abstractions. We call them the "poor." I've heard the marginalized and the displaced referred to as "those people." How can we break loose from language, actions, and mindsets that dehumanize the very people we want to serve? The answer is proximity. Theologian Gustavo Gutiérrez is credited with saying, "You say you care about the poor. Then tell me, what are their names?"

MY NEIGHBORS, MY 'HOOD

I lived in the same 'hood in Oakland for the better part of the past ten years. When the landlord sold my building, I had to move on. It was a sad time. When I first moved onto that block, I was a stranger. I'll never forget the day I had to move out eight years later. Neighbors were in and out of my house helping with boxes and furniture.

In the midst of the foot traffic, there was a knock at the door. One of my neighbors (a meth addict who lived in the back seat of an abandoned car across the street) was there with a friend who was dealing with some domestic abuse problems. They wanted prayer. It wasn't just a sad day for me, it was a sad day for them as well. I was the pastor of that 'hood, not because I came outside with the bullhorn thundering Scriptures out of a well-worn King James Bible. We had shared the journey of life together. Some days it simply consisted of, "What's up, Rev?" And some days it was, "My child ain't come home in three days. Can we just pray right here on the sidewalk?"

When my neighbors saw me walking down the street, they'd offer a ride. Once, I was wrestling with gout and arthritis and could barely walk. One of the neighbors grabbed my groceries with one hand and almost carried me home. The day thieves broke into my apartment, one of my neighbors risked his life to run them off. I will never forget his kindness. It came after years of merely saying, "What's up?"

Trust is earned. It literally took a few years before people realized that the preacher down the block is someone who can keep his mouth shut. That level of trust put me in the position to stop someone from giving an enemy a one-way trip to the cemetery. Sometimes it simply came down to being in the right place at the right moment.

Go back to the Gospels. How many of Jesus' interactions occurred through presence? He just happened to be walking or sitting somewhere and ran into someone God had preordained him to meet. Often, this took place in some out of the way places like the meeting between our Lord and the woman at the well. Consider the story of the Samaritan and the mugging victim or the Samaritan walking down the dangerous Jericho Road. So much of ministry is proximity. It's about being present.

The Christian Community Development Association (CCDA) is a well-known organization that believes people need to live where they serve. They call this *incarnational ministry*. Just as Jesus was incarnated as a native of Israel, the incarnated person becomes a part of the place being served. No longer outsiders, incarnated ministers have thrown their lot in with the people who live in the community. The CCDA believes that calls for a long-term commitment.

There is something to the phrase *incarnational ministry*. As a resident of the city where I do most of my ministry, I am known. Notice, I said *known*, not "famous." Two years after I left my previous apartment, I was sitting in a burrito shop, and a woman walked in and said, "Hey, you don't live around here anymore."

I was somewhat startled because I didn't know her from Eve.

She said, "I lived in the building right behind you and I've seen you around here for years."

Speaking of the burrito shop, I have eaten at the same place on High Street for years. They make great burritos, but no one in there speaks a word of English apart from the menu items. Yet when I walk in, they say, "Hola!" and I feel a sense of belonging there. I don't drive to this 'hood, deliver my twenty-minute sermon, and then flee for the suburbs. This is my home, and it makes all of the difference when I have a conversation with someone. It is key. Being present was a key to Jesus' ministry. It will work for you too.

THE PRESENCE OF LIGHT AND PROXIMITY

When I was young, I was taught that to be a Christian is to verbally share the Word of God or at the very least to give out gospel tracts. My thinking on that has changed over the years. As a believer, each morning when we walk outside our front doors, whether we're conscious of it or not, we are light in a sprawling expanse of darkness. We are kindness in a world where drivers cut us off in hopes of gaining a ten-second advantage on the way to the stop sign up the street. We are the presence of grace reflecting Christ in a dog-eat-rat world. Just walking from one side of the street to the other can be ministry.

In the red words of the Gospels attributed to Jesus, we find a call to nonconformity. We find a summons to a life that demands we make an impact for the kingdom of God. In Jesus' words, we find no room for apathy or lethargy. In Matthew 5:13, Jesus said that the body of Christ is to be the salt of the earth. One ingredient that can make an expensive cut of meat burst with flavor: salt. Salt brings out the flavor in most foods. It adds a zest. Salt changes everything. Salt doesn't only enhance taste, it acts as a preservative. Jesus is saying that a mighty difference should be made when a believer spends time somewhere. The whole situation changes when we are there.

Jesus goes on to say, "You are the light of the world. A town built on a hill cannot be hidden" (Matthew 5:14). Oakland is about twenty minutes from midtown San Francisco. At night, people at a good vantage point can see the beautiful San Francisco skyline ablaze in the glory of the lights shining from its tall buildings. Is that what Jesus meant for us, that our witness as the church should be so astounding that it couldn't be missed from miles away? As the light of the world, we are called to glow in the darkness.

God uses us as God chooses. When we go into the world as ambassadors for Jesus Christ—as salt and light—God might use us to open a door for someone whose hands are filled with shopping bags. God might use us to look at someone studying for an exam in a coffee shop and say, "Hang in there. You're going to do well." God might use us to hold a conversation with a lonely person with mental illness.

I was on a bus a few weeks ago when an elderly gentleman fell asleep with his head on my shoulder. Moments later, he woke up, turned to me in slight embarrassment, and said, "Thank you." Since God is sending me out to be salt and light, I need to recognize that those interactions are just as important to God as the opportunities that I might get to preach on a Sunday morning.

Not long ago, a woman sitting in a wheelchair in front of a supermarket hollered to me, a total stranger. She said, "Excuse me! Mister, I'm hungry! Would you buy me some milk and some oatmeal?" *Ahh, here,* I thought, *is my opportunity to be light in the darkness, to serve as Jesus in the world that needs his touch.*

I treated that occasion with all of the solemnity and sanctity that I would treat the preparation and delivery of a sermon.

Some days God calls on me to preach a sermon to a thousand people. Some days, God calls on me to go get some groceries for the lady in a wheelchair. Is one act of obedience less than the other? No. By saying hi to that businessperson or the homeless couple with the weight of the world on their shoulders, we are serving God. We may have been placed on that bus to offer an elderly person a seat.

And please don't discount the ministry of prayer. Pray for the people who approach you as you walked down the street. Pray for the barista at Starbucks. Say a silent prayer for the person sitting next to you on the bus or in the doctor's office. They may never know what you're doing, but God hears. And those people need the blessing of intercession on their behalf.

To walk down the street praying to the Creator in a world where principalities and powers of darkness surround God's creatures is a powerful act of resistance.

TOP OF THE MORNING

This conscious decision to partner with the Creator in the construction of our day must be coupled with the act of surrender of our will. The Christian's day must begin with a petition to be used for God's glory. We must be fully aware of being God's vessel before stepping outside each morning.

A black and white photo hangs on my living room wall. It is a close-up of a child's hand enveloped in the huge hand of its parent. Both are wearing overcoats, so we can assume they are outside. I purchased that image because it is the picture of the evangelist's walk with God. It is a picture not only of a trained missionary headed toward a foreign land but of you and me walking to the corner store for a quart of ice cream.

Does every human interaction we have between breakfast and bedtime have eternal significance? The older I get, the easier it is to look in the rearview mirror and see that apparently random occurrences actually have divinely ordered steps. The thing is to walk in the world curious, aware, and open to the fact that God, who is alive in our lives and ablaze in the world, has not only commanded us to be salt and light but also seeks to lead us to places where we can be just that.

MAY I ASK FOR YOUR PERMISSION?

Cesar Cruz is a legend in Oakland. This Harvard-educated visionary and cofounder of Homies Empowerment, an organization that embraces gang-involved youth and offers them healing and a path to college, taught me to approach people by saying, "May I ask for your permission?" They are words of grace. They acknowledge the humanity and dignity of the individual on the other end of your words. People going through a state of homelessness and the formerly incarcerated are used to having people in authority trample their personal boundaries. They are used to being taught *at* and talked down to like toddlers with hearing issues. Recognizing that, before I dump sermons on people or offer advice, I respect people enough to ask if it's all right to speak into their lives.

Rather than go into a theological treatise about the leading of God in the life of the urban Christian servant, I will share three distinct times when I not only felt but saw the leading of God in interactions that took place over a five-day period.

Tuesday morning. "Hey! How 'bout those A's!" she shouted across the restaurant.

It took me a minute to realize that the young woman with the silky black hair was actually hollering at me.

"Oh, right!" I said, glancing down at the big, green A's symbol on my shirt. "They are doing pretty good."

What was I saying? I haven't watched a baseball game yet this season. *Forgive me, Lord.*

Well, that should have been the end of the conversation, civil pleasantries exchanged in a crowded fast-food restaurant between two perfect strangers. But, no, it wasn't.

"Those A's are rocking it. They're hot with the bat this year!"

I smiled rather uncomfortably at this point. She didn't notice, or if she did, my discomfort didn't slow her down. She started shouting out batting averages and pitching rotations. How to tell her that I'm not really a big baseball fan? I hunted for a clean shirt that matched the pants I'd be wearing this morning, and now here we are. That was really the extent of my commitment to the hometown team.

Finally, the lady behind the counter with the McDonald's logo on her cap called my number. I took a deep breath as she handed me my Egg McMuffin, hash brown patties, and soda. My new baseball buddy was now tied up at the counter getting her order. I smiled pleasantly enough and then found my way to a seat in the back, close to the door.

Well, that was that, I thought. I took off my black Oakland Raiders hat, said grace, and dug into breakfast. I took a bite out of the hash browns and almost went into cardiogenic shock. Someone must have dumped half a container of Morton's salt on that thing. I tried to wash the gritty taste away with some soda. It was flat. The breakfast sandwich must have been left over from last year's "Everything Must Go" sale. It tasted, well, old.

As I sat there contemplating how McDonald's had failed me, I heard a chair scrape across the floor. I had a dining guest.

"So you think the A's will make it to the World Series?"

I almost laughed. There was a sweetness about her, a twinkle in her eye. Turns out that her granddad had been a big A's fan. He used to take her to the games. There was a note of sadness, of loss, in her voice when she spoke of him. It took just a few words to understand the depth of her love for him. I wondered if anyone else in life had loved her as he had. Later, it came to me. I was probably her grandfather's age. Perhaps he'd even had a belly and salt-and-pepper hair like I do. Perhaps something about me reminded her of Granddad.

At one point in the conversation (which was more like a monologue), she accentuated some point by stretching her arms open wide. I almost gasped at what I saw. I told myself not to stare or allow the shock to show on my face. It was her left inner arm. Ugly, inch-long scars raced up and down like railroad tracks made by a madman. They were thick and discolored. I've seen marks made with razor blades by people with cutting issues, but this looked like someone had gouged out chunks of flesh from her arm with a hatchet. I watched closely as her right arm rose. The same thing.

2222

22222222222222222

She had her food bagged to go. She just sat down to speak to me for one more moment.

"Well, I have to get back to work," she said. I would never have asked her where. I never pry. Most of the time, I let folks share only what they wish to reveal. For some reason though, she told me.

"I work at a gentlemen's club," she said.

That one phrase could overload the internet. She spends her days and nights in a dark room where women are treated like fresh pieces of meat, less than nothing, to be pawed at and disposed of by wealthy patrons who leave the din of darkness and despair only to walk through the door of a baby mansion in the suburbs and say to some sad, lonely wife, "Hey, honey, what's for dinner?"

When she left the restaurant, this young woman, who couldn't have been more than twenty-five, would allow herself to be propositioned by men who treat her as a species lower than humanity. Part of her "job" today would consist of keeping men she didn't know from pinching her breasts and bottom uninvited.

Why did she engage me in conversation? Perhaps it was the relief of having a real conversation with a man who looked into her eyes without raking her over from shoulder to shoe. Perhaps it was the chance to enjoy a few moments of chitchat with someone who made her feel human again, who might have even reminded her of Granddad, the one man who treated her with kindness without wanting something from her.

How did she know it was safe to talk to me? When a woman spends her life in the company of men who use and discard her, it can't be difficult to know when someone is looking at her with a different set of eyes. It probably took her as long as it is taking you to read this sentence to sense in her soul that I was safe. The Oakland A's were simply a way to cross a barrier between strangers. After a few minutes more of conversation, she picked up her food. She smiled broadly, wished me a nice day, and walked out of the restaurant.

Wednesday. My friend Pastor Albert Lee let me out of his car near the corner of MacArthur and Fruitvale Avenue in Oakland. My stomach was full. He and I had just filled our bellies at Lena's Soul Food restaurant. The dining fare of fried chicken, macaroni, and collard greens had me walking just a few steps slower than usual. A heavyset African American woman with the top of her Afro dyed purple cut me off. She closed in until we were almost nose to nose.

"Would you pray for me, sir?"

I didn't recognize her. I meet a lot of people in my comings and goings, but I think I would have remembered a middle-age woman with her hair dyed purple.

I stopped walking and shut out the bustle of the thick foot traffic and honking horns. My mind was totally transfixed on her need.

"What do you want us to pray about?"

She said, "I'm hungry. I want you to pray that God would send me a meal."

I tend to be on the mystical side. Could it be that God was saying, *I just fed you so much food that you want to go somewhere and sleep it off. What's to be done for this child of mine?*

"What do you want to eat?"

She pointed at a Chinese takeout spot across the street.

I said, "Let's go."

Like I said earlier, I don't ask a lot of questions. It's rude to intrude into someone's personal life. However, she volunteered. She was just coming home from the penitentiary. Sister was serving some of her time at a half-way house in the community. She goes to church sometimes, I learned as we walked together.

I have missed meals from time to time when things got tough. However, I would be hard-pressed to say that I actually knew hunger. But this sister knew hunger. I could tell from the way her eyes spread open when I opened the door of the Chinese restaurant and the aroma of the beef and broccoli rushed out to meet us. She hurried to the counter.

"Get what you want, sister."

Those words did not need to be repeated. She pointed at three different items on the hot tray to go with her fried rice. Then she asked for an AriZona iced tea.

There was only one thing missing. I had neglected to say the prayer she'd requested. But did I need to? She wanted prayer for food, and five minutes later, there it was, so much of it that she'd need both hands to carry the tray.

Should I have said the prayer? Was I being overly religious? Whatever. Right after the food was rung up and the sum placed on my debit card, I said, "C'mon sister, let's pray." She grabbed both hands, and we prayed. And then, it was just like I was invisible to her. I could dig it. Sister was hungry. She rushed to an open table and plunged in a fork. I think she might have said, "God bless you!" as I walked out.

Saturday. I watched him stumble and swerve across a busy street like he was in a walking coma. For a moment I thought he was going to fall face-down on the asphalt. At which point, being that I am a minister, I'd have to go help him. *Oh, Lord, help him!* I prayed silently.

Ahh, he made it to the sidewalk. He almost walked right into me. I looked back later, and he was sitting on the sidewalk. I waited at the bus stop, glancing back him occasionally as I checked my Facebook posts. Ten minutes later, he was laid out on the sidewalk as if he were asleep or . . .

An elderly couple walked up to him. He lay there at toe level, motionless. They eyed him for a couple of minutes. They looked both ways and then crossed the street, like the priest and the Levite on the Jericho Road.

Was he drunk? Was he high? Was he in a diabetic coma? Should I go over and see about him; maybe take his pulse (or try). Being that I have no medical training at all, I don't know if that would have helped him. There was one thing I could do to help him. If the Samaritan in Jesus' famous parable owned one of the things that most twenty-first-century Americans do, the story would have ended differently. I pulled out my cell phone and called 9-1-1. Soon sirens were blaring. Red lights were flashing. Medical professionals were on the scene.

Looking back at those three interactions brought one more thing to mind. Each of those people was a different ethnicity. One was black. One was white. One was Latino. The couple who leaned over to look at the man splayed out on the sidewalk were Asian immigrants. What might God have been saying by including such diversity in these stories?

LIVING THE EVERYDAY LIFE OF PROXIMITY

All three stories I just recounted have one thing in common. I didn't come across those three people in a church building. I didn't plan to meet any of them. I connected with each one as I was traveling from point A to point B in the inner city. Each was suffering and needed a touch from God. In each case I was able to administer that salve. I offered the lady at McDonald's a listening ear in what might have been a difficult moment. I offered a meal to the woman at the corner of Fruitvale and MacArthur Boulevard when she was hungry. I was in the right place at just the right time to summon the medical care that might have saved a man's life.

Does that mean I'm someone special, different from you? Hardly. God, the grand Architect of the universe, placed me in just the right place and time to make a difference. It didn't take much to help any of those people. I was simply in the lane where our paths could intersect.

Not every interaction God creates in your day will be followed by fireworks and marching bands. Sure, sometimes the Spirit leads us to people ready and willing to surrender their lives to Christ with tears and trembling. Sometimes the Holy Spirit might lead us to an intersection where our mission is to pick up the front of a single mother's baby stroller as she struggles to get on a bus. There are no big deeds and small ones. There is only obedience in the all-seeing eye of God.

I grew up going to Sunday school. One of the stories taught from the Bible has had a profound impact on my life. Acts 8:26 says, "An angel of the Lord said to Philip, 'Go south to the road—the desert road—that goes down from Jerusalem to Gaza.'" Notice, the angel spoke to Philip and told him to go to the middle of nowhere. No further instructions are given. Philip only gets that one play drawn in the sand. He surrenders to the will of God. And then in the desert, his life intersects with a high government official from what would be modern-day Sudan. Here, Philip's obedient footsteps land him in the path of someone who will convert to Christ and then bring the gospel of Jesus to sub-Saharan Africa.

Why did God choose Philip? Maybe because Philip didn't ask any questions. He just heard the command and went.

I have a friend who is successful in the entertainment industry. He and I were driving in Los Angeles one day when I asked him for one of his keys to success. He said, "You don't have any control over when something will happen, but you can put yourself in places where it is likely to happen." Urban ministry works basically the same way. I don't sit in an office and wait for people to walk into the church asking for help. I go to where they are, and God creates the times and spaces where things occur.

Being present in the community is the best possible learning tool. Talk to the server in the coffee shop. Start a conversation with people sitting next to you at the burrito shop. Leave your car at home and take the bus. Look for opportunities to volunteer at after-school programs or literacy programs at the library. Slip into a storefront church during services in the 'hood. Listen to the words between the words. Be an observer. Journey with people. Don't pretend to show up with the answers, because the real experts are people who have lived in that neighborhood or neighborhoods like it since birth.

SEEING THE THINGS GOD IS SHOWING US

When I walked across the parking lot of my favorite burrito spot the other day, I noticed one of my neighbors, "Louie," standing between parked cars. Louie always speaks to me. If I'm two blocks away and he can see me, he'll holler "Rev!" Something was different this day. Louie didn't say anything as he watched me approach. In fact, his eyes cut in a different direction entirely. And then I saw something I might not have noticed had I not learned how to really see when in the 'hood.

A man in a long, white T-shirt walked up to Louie. Louie barely looked at him as they slapped hands. They didn't exchange a word. The man kept walking. Louie was selling drugs. He didn't speak to me because he was ashamed and didn't want me to see that part of his life.

I went into the burrito spot, ordered my food, and sat at the window. Several more people walked up to Louie; none stayed an appreciable length of time. And then a black and white Crown Victoria pulled alongside the building that housed the restaurant. I looked at the officer and almost chuckled. Louie has probably been doing this since he was ten. He's not going to get arrested by a uniformed officer in a police car. As soon as I had that thought, Louie became invisible.

Louie is someone I can have a real conversation with. He's the kind of person that might walk up to me and ask me to pray about his mama. How can the parking lot incident help me to share a word with Louie? How might it strengthen my prayers for him? Instead of giving Louie vague, amorphous advice laced with Bible verses, one day I might be in a place to warn Louie about prison and the fact that he might be under surveillance. Perhaps I am the only person he'd listen to. Is it possible that God placed me at that particular spot at that particular time for a reason? If you are not a part of the community, you are not going to meet Louie, let alone be in a place to help keep him out of prison or share the way of eternal life. Louie's not going to let people he doesn't know into his life. So if you want to share the good news of the gospel with homies, they have to get to know you and vice versa.

THE POWER OF PROXIMITY

In her book *The Power of Proximity*, author Michelle Ferrigno Warren writes:

> Becoming proximate to the poor, those impacted most by injustice, is the most radical, transformative thing you can do to affect it. Proximity is powerful. Learning about injustice from a book or from a short-term experience may tug at the strings of your heart, but it offers a very limited view.... Studying theology, sociology, anthropology, or policy is also a great way to build your foundation as a person who can affect issues. But these actions are still limited. They keep you on the back of the bus away from the action.... In contrast, proximity to injustice transforms your view of the bigger world and the people moving around in it. More importantly, it transforms you in all the ways necessary to help you take part in God's process of redeeming and rebuilding what is broken.[2]

If Jesus had spent all of his ministry preaching inside the temple, you'd have never heard of him. He would have died of old age.

He waged the resistance in the streets and back roads of ancient Palestine. He was even crucified publicly.

Much of the Bible reveals a Savior who was out among the people he loved. In Luke 19:10, Jesus celebrated the repentance of a known thug and hustler with the words, "The Son of Man came to seek and to save the lost." The word *seek* is critical to our understanding of the passage. You can't do a whole lot of seeking inside a building. Jesus says he came looking for people like Zacchaeus, the most hated and feared individual in the 'hood (Luke 19:7). If the church was committed to living out the principles left to us in verse 10, what would our churches look like in the future? How would they transform? How would the resistance against stifling tradition and apathy affect the way we go forward as the resistance? The answers lie with you.

HOMEWORK

- What are the three greatest ways this book challenged you? How do you plan to meet these challenges?

- What are some ideas from this book that you could implement right away in your own journey?

NOTES

3: CHILDREN OF THE STREETS

[1]Constance Rice, *Power Concedes Nothing* (New York: Scribner's, 2012), 146.

[2]Michael Pfleger, "Ignoring Black Teens Is a Form of Abortion," *YouTube*, accessed January 22, 2019, www.youtube.com/watch?v=TCDJEnE42I0&feature=youtu.be.

[3]Jiwe Morris, "Do you know how many kids grow up gutter, crack babies because the daddy's a gangster who promotes violence?" Facebook, 2017. Used by permission.

[4]Nicia De'Lovely, phone interview with the author, July 13, 2018.

[5]De'Lovely, interview with the author.

4: GENTRIFICATION

[1]Maria Poblet, "The Struggle for the Flatlands: How Oakland Can Fight Gentrification," Causa Justa: Just Cause, accessed January 22, 2019, https://cjjc.org/publication/the-struggle-for-the-flatlands-how-oakland-can-fight-gentrification.

[2]Harry Williams, "Back to the Scene of the Crime," YouTube, January 16, 2015, www.youtube.com/watch?v=TE7cbeMTL3E&feature=youtu.be.

[3]*Brother from Another Planet*, directed by John Sayles (New York: Cinecom Pictures, 1984).

5: CROSSING CULTURES

[1]Ken Hardy, speech delivered at a San Francisco YMCA conference, 2018.

[2]Hardy, YMCA conference, 2018.

[3]Willie Lynch, "Willie Lynch Letter 1712," Internet Archive, December 25, 1712, https://archive.org/details/WillieLynch Letter1712.

[4]Joy DeGruy, *Post Traumatic Slave Syndrome* (Portland, OR: Joy DeGruy Publications, 2005), 107-8.

[5]Jamie Taylor, face-to-face interview with the author, July 23, 2018.

6: DEATH IN THE POT

[1]Eric B. and Rakim, "In the Ghetto," *Let the Rhythm Hit 'Em*, MCA Records, New York, 1990.

[2]Muhammad Ali, quoted in Thomas Hauser, "The Thoughts of Muhammad Ali in Exile," *History Is a Weapon*, accessed October 30, 2018, www.historyisaweapon.com/defcon1 /hauser.html.

[3]"Passion of the Ruckus," *The Boondocks*, season 1, episode 15, directed by Seung Eun Kim, written by Aaron McGruder, aired March 19, 2006, on Adult Swim.

[4]Jomo Kenyatta, quoted in "Jomo Kenyatta on the Arrival of Christianity in Kenya," Georgetown University, accessed October 30, 2018, https://berkleycenter.georgetown.edu /quotes/jomo-kenyatta-on-the-arrival-of-christianity-in-kenya.

[5]John Henrik Clarke, *A Great and Mighty Walk*, directed by St. Clair Bourne, written by Lou Potter, Black Dot Media, 1996.

[6]John Henrik Clarke, "Christianity Before Christ," Originalpeople .org, accessed October 30, 2018, http://originalpeople.org /christianity-before-christ-dr-john-henrik-clarke.

[7]John Henrik Clarke, quoted in Dr. John Henrik Clarke— January 1, 1915—July 16, 1998, YSDWYSD.com, January 4, 2013, www.ysdwysd.com/gallery/john-henrik-clarke-remembered.

[8]William Moseley, *What Color Was Jesus?* (Chicago: African-American Images, 1987), 33.

[9]Edward J. Blum and Paul Harvey, *The Color of Christ: The Son of God and the Saga of Race in America* (Chapel Hill: University of North Carolina Press, 2014).

[10]J. A. Rogers, *Africa's Gift to America* (New York: Helga M. Rogers, 1989), 9.

[11]Rogers, *Africa's Gift to America*, 11.

[12]Yosef A.A. Ben-Jochannan, *Africa: Mother of Western Civilization* (Baltimore: Black Classics, 1988), 195.

[13]Dale Brown, ed., *Africa's Glorious Legacy* (Alexandria, VA: Time-Life Books, 1994), 43.

[14]Henry T. Aubin, *The Rescue of Jerusalem* (New York: Soho Press, 2002), 133, 141-42.

[15]Walter Arthur McCray, *The Black Presence in the Bible* (Chicago: Black Light Fellowship, 1990), 71.

[16]Marty Grace, *Don't Call Me Black Because I'm a Spirit* (New York: Welstar, 1987), vi.

[17]Grace, *Don't Call Me Black*, 40, 38.

[18]Malcolm X, quoted in Adrienne Maree Brown, "By Any Means Necessary," *Yes!* magazine, May 20, 2010.

[19]Manning Marable, *Malcolm X: A Life of Reinvention* (New York: Viking Press, 2011), 71.

[20]Malcolm X, quoted in Alex Haley, "An Interview with Malcolm X," *Playboy*, May 1963.

[21]Malcolm X with Alex Haley, *The Autobiography of Malcolm X* (New York: Ballantine, 1964), 253, 277-78.

[22]Malcolm X, "History Is a Weapon," historyisaweapon.com, accessed January 22, 2019, www.historyisaweapon.com /defcon1/malconafamhist.html.

[23]Malcolm X, "History Is a Weapon."

[24]Malcolm X, quoted in George Breitmann, *Malcolm X Speaks* (New York: Grove Press, 1994), 168.

[25]Malcolm X, quoted in James Cone, *Martin & Malcolm & America* (Maryknoll, NY: Orbis Books, 1995), 107.

[26]Ossie Davis, eulogy delivered at the funeral of Malcolm X, Faith Temple Church of God, February 27, 1965, http://malcolmx .com/eulogy.

7: TRUE RELIGION

[1]Albert J. Raboteau, *A Fire in the Bones* (Boston: Beacon Press, 1995), 18.

[2]Richard Allen, quoted in *The Life, Experience and Gospel Labors of the Rt. Richard Allen*, 1833, The Making of the African-American Identity, vol. 1 (1500-1865), National Humanities Resource Tool Box, nationalhumanitiescenter.org/pds/livingrev/religion/text7/allen.pdf.

[3]Henry Highland Garnet, quoted in *African American Religion*, ed. Timothy E. Fulop and Albert J. Raboteau (Oxford: Oxford University Press, 1999), 37.

[4]Peter J. Paris, *The Social Teaching of the Black Churches* (Philadelphia: Fortress Press, 1985), 12.

[5]Ralph Abernathy, *And the Walls Came Tumbling Down* (New York: Harper & Row, 1989), 149-50.

[6]Abernathy, *And the Walls Came Tumbling Down*, 149.

[7]J. Alfred Smith Sr., phone interview with the author, 2018.

[8]Howard Thurman, *Jesus and the Disinherited* (Boston: Beacon Press, 1976), 14-15.

[9]Thurman, *Jesus and the Disinherited*, 13.

[10]Thurman, *Jesus and the Disinherited*, 13.

8: SOCIAL JUSTICE

[1]David Simon, "There Are Now Two Americas," *The Observer*, December 7, 2013, www.theguardian.com/world/2013/dec/08/david-simon-capitalism-marx-two-americas-wire.

[2]Max Ehrenfreund, "17 Disturbing Statistics from Federal Report on Ferguson Police," *Washington Post*, March 4, 2015, www.washingtonpost.com/news/wonk/wp/2015/03/04/17-disturbing-statistics-from-the-federal-report-on-ferguson-police/?noredirect=on&utm_term=.47b51685c025.

[3]Alex Shashkevich, "Police Officers Speak Less Respectfully to Black Residents Than to White Residents, Stanford Researchers Find," *Stanford News*, June 5, 2017, https://news.stanford.edu/press-releases/2017/06/05/cops-speak-less-community-members.

[4]Brad Heath, "Racial Gap in U.S. Arrest Rates: 'Staggering Disparity,'" *USA Today*, November 19, 2014, www.usatoday.com/story/news/nation/2014/11/18/ferguson-black-arrest-rates/19043207.

[5]Dora Lind, "The FBI Is Trying to Get Better Data on Police Killings," *Vox*, April 10, 2015, www.vox.com/2014/8/21/6051043/how-many -people-killed-police-statistics-homicide-official-black.

[6]Tawanda Jones, phone interview with the author, May 20, 2016. The remainder of the Tyrone West story is based on this interview.

[7]Rick Perez, phone interview with the author, February 23, 2017. The remainder of the Pedie Perez story is based on this interview.

[8]Jeralynn Brown-Blueford, phone interview with the author, February 24, 2017. The remainder of the Alan Blueford story is based on this interview.

[9]Mitchell Duneier, *Ghetto: The Invention of a Place, the History of an Idea* (New York: Farrar, Straus & Giroux, 2016), xi-xii.

[10]James Braxton Peterson, *Prison Industrial Complex for Beginners* (Danbury, CT: For Beginners Publishing, 2016), 3.

[11]"Shadow Report to the United Nations on Racial Disparities in the United States Criminal Justice System," *Sentencing Project*, August 31, 2013, www.sentencingproject.org/publications /shadow-report-to-the-united-nations-human-rights -committee-regarding-racial-disparities-in-the-united-states -criminal-justice-system.

[12]James Kilgore, *Understanding Mass Incarceration* (New York: New Press, 2015), 12.

[13]Bob Dylan, "Sweetheart Like You," *Infidels*, Columbia Records, 1983.

[14]Kilgore, *Understanding Mass Incarceration*, 14.

[15]2Pac, "My Block," *Better Dayz*, Interscope Records, 2002.

[16]Michael McLaughlin, "Felon Voting Laws Disenfranchise 5.85 Million Americans with Criminal Records: The Sentencing Project," *Huffington Post*, July 12, 2012, www.huffingtonpost .com/2012/07/12/felon-voting-laws-disenfranchise-sentencing -project_n_1665860.html.

[17]Michelle Alexander, *The New Jim Crow* (New York: New Press, 2010), 177.

[18]Ice Cube, "When I Get To Heaven" (skit), *Lethal Injection*, Interscope Records, 1993.

[19]Martin Luther King Jr., *A Testament of Hope* (New York: Harper Collins, 1986), 346.

[20]Brown-Blueford, interview with the author.

9: THE RISE OF THE PROSPERITY GOSPEL

[1]Arthur Huff Fauset, *Black Gods of the Metropolis* (Philadelphia: University of Pennsylvania, 1971), 24.

[2]Marie W. Dallam, *Daddy Grace: A Celebrity Preacher and His House of Prayer* (New York: New York University Press, 2007), 1.

[3]Fauset, *Black Gods of the Metropolis*, 26.

[4]Dallam, *Daddy Grace*, 88.

[5]Fauset, *Black Gods of the Metropolis*, 22.

[6]John Painter, *1, 2 and 3 John* (Collegeville, MN: Liturgical Press, 2002), 367.

[7]C. S. Lewis, *The Problem of Pain* (New York: Touchstone, 1997), 35.

[8]Skip Moen, phone interview with the author, March 1, 2018.

[9]Jim Jones, quoted in John Jacobs and Tim Reiterman, *Raven* (New York: E. P. Dutton, 1982), 149.

[10]Julia Scheeres, *A Thousand Lives* (New York: Simon & Schuster, 2011), 228.

10: RETHINKING URBAN MINISTRY

[1]Adam Clayton Powell Jr., *Adam by Adam* (New York: Kensington, 1971), 57.

[2]Powell, *Adam by Adam*, 57-58.

[3]"Jamal Bryant G CHECKED by PFK BOOM and Shy Lady Heroin," YouTube, accessed January 22, 2019, https://youtube/J_ECdKuAgxo.

[4]PFK Boom (Devon Neverdon), phone interview with the author, June 25, 2016.

11: WAGING PEACE

[1]Malik Spellman, phone interview with the author, April 5, 2018. The remainder of Spellman's story is taken from this interview.

12: STORIES FROM THE STREETS

[1]Michael Pfleger, phone interview with the author, December 3, 2018. The remainder of Father Mike's story is taken from this interview.

[2]Michael Pfleger, "What Does It Mean to Be a Voice of Conscience?" YouTube, November 9, 2010. www.youtube.com/watch?v=Ogv7fWOE8G4.

[3]Pfleger, interview with the author.

[4]Joseph Jones, interview with the author, 2018. The remainder of Rev. Jones's story is taken from this interview.

[5]Larry Austin, face-to-face interview with the author, 2018. The remainder of Pastor Larry's story is taken from this interview.

[6]Regina Evans, phone interview with the author, April 23, 2017. The remainder of Regina's story is taken from this interview.

13: PROXIMITY

[1]*Bronx Tale*, directed by Robert De Niro, written by Chazz Palminteri (New York: TriBeCa Productions, 1993).

[2]Michelle Ferrigno Warren, *The Power of Proximity* (Downers Grove, IL: InterVarsity Press, 2017), 8.